Flexible Learning in Higher Education

EDITED BY
**Winnie Wade, Keith Hodgkinson,
Alison Smith and John Arfield**

**KOGAN
PAGE**

London ● Philadelphia

First published in 1994

Apart from any fair dealing for the purposes of research or private study, or criticism or review, as permitted under the Copyright, Designs and Patents Act, 1988, this publication may only be reproduced, stored or transmitted, in any form or by any means, with the prior permission in writing of the publishers, or in the case of reprographic reproduction in accordance with the terms of licences issued by the Copyright Licensing Agency. Enquiries concerning reproduction outside those terms should be sent to the publishers at the undermentioned address:

Kogan Page Limited
120 Pentonville Road
London N1 9JN

© Wade, Hodgkinson, Smith, Arfield and named contributors, 1994

British Library Cataloguing in Publication Data
A CIP record for this book is available from the British Library.

ISBN 0 7494 1418 9

Typeset by Saxon Graphics Ltd, Derby

Printed and bound in Great Britain by Biddles Ltd,
Guildford and King's Lynn.

Contents

The Contributors

John Arfield has been university librarian at Loughborough University of Technology since 1992. Previously, he worked in university libraries in Cambridge, Cardiff and Reading. He has a particular interest in using information technology to support student learning.

Jonathan Beaverstock is currently a lecturer in economic geography in the department of geography, Loughborough University of Technology. His research interests focus on labour market restructuring and migration within the world cities and the role of service industries in Britain. At present he is the director of a Nuffield Foundation social science project examining economic regeneration in Coalville, North-West Leicestershire. Previously, he has held research positions in the school of advanced urban studies and the department of geography, University of Bristol.

Ed Brown is a lecturer in the department of geography at Loughborough University of Technology where he specializes in the political and economic geography of the Central American region and third world development issues more generally. He is also the coordinator of the Flexible Learning Initiative in the geography department at LUT.

Richard Clark is the flexible learning officer at Loughborough University of Technology. Richard has worked in the area of student representation for several years, both as an undergraduate course representative and as a part-time and then full-time sabbatical officer for Loughborough Students' Union. In this role he pioneered developments in enhancing student representation through the training of student officers in a number of institutions. He now works in the Flexible Learning Initiative focusing on the learning support needs of Loughborough University's undergraduate community.

John Costello is associate dean (teaching) in the school of education and humanities at Loughborough University. He is involved in the development of modular programmes and of credit accumulation systems leading to degree awards, as well as in planning the future structure of the academic year.

Joyce Cubitt has been a part-time lecturer in the department of design and technology at Loughborough University of Technology over the past ten years with responsibility for technology teaching on different courses. She was one of the authors of *Advanced Design and Technology* recently published by Longman (in her previous name of Riley). She is at present researching and producing flexible learning material in design and technology.

Keith Hodgkinson is senior lecturer in education. Keith taught history in a Nottinghamshire secondary school before moving to Loughborough to teach history methodology and multicultural education. He is now the PGCE primary course tutor and has published on history and humanities teaching, information technology and primary teacher training.

Tony Hodgson has substantial experience in the field of design and technology education, and has been actively involved in the promotion of design-based teaching in secondary schools. Following appointments as head of design faculty in school, he concentrated on initial teacher training and INSET work at Sheffield City Polytechnic, moving to Loughborough University of Technology in 1992. His main areas of research interests are concerned with the use of information technology in design education, and the technological requirements of designers. Consultancy work has included the development of industrial computer control systems and educational software applications.

Brian Jarvis is a lecturer in American literature in the department of English and drama at Loughborough. He teaches courses on nineteenth and twentieth century American writing, film and critical theory. His primary research interest is in the representation of place in contemporary American culture.

Peter Lewis is a lecturer in the department of mathematical sciences at Loughborough University with considerable experience of teaching large classes, particularly of engineers. His main interests are in the teaching and learning of applied and applicable mathematics in higher education. He is the co-author of two undergraduate textbooks and is also a tutor for the Open University.

Eddie Norman is a lecturer in the department of design and technology at Loughborough University of Technology. Current primary research interests centre on the use of scientific knowledge and concepts in design activity, with numerous associated publications. He made a major contribution to the textbook *Advanced Design and Technology*, recently published by Longman, and edited *Teaching Design and Technology 5–16*, which explored the Leicestershire design model as an approach to teaching National Curriculum technology. He was also co-author of a video series aimed at key stage 3 design and technology.

Alison Smith is deputy director of management development and director of professional programmes at Loughborough University Business School. Previously a lecturer in further education involved in both vocational training and academic programmes, she is currently employed on the design, direction and delivery of post-experience management development programmes for corporate and public sector clients. She has published widely in both national and international management journals and regularly presents at conferences both in the UK and abroad.

Winnie Wade coordinates the Flexible Learning Initiative at Loughborough University of Technology and is directing the HEFC national dissemination programme for the 'Flexibility in Course Provision' projects. She has extensive teaching and staff development experience in higher education and has published widely.

Phil Wild, lecturer in education, has a long background in advisory work in information technology and science teaching in Gloucestershire. He is now responsible for supporting the IT requirements of both staff and students within the education department at Loughborough, as well as being responsible for the physics PGCE students.

Ian Wright is a senior lecturer in the Engineering Design Institute at Loughborough University of Technology. He has been involved in the design and production of flexible learning programmes since the mid-1980s. He managed a large Open Tech project and associated funding from the Design Council to produce continuing education packages for managers of computer aided engineering systems. More recently, he has developed flexible learning material for the training of engineers at companies like Rolls Royce and British Aerospace.

Foreword

In 1992, the Universities Funding Council, immediate forerunner of the present Higher Education Funding Council, promoted its specially funded programme Flexibility in Course Provision (FCP) in Higher Education. Universities submitted projects which would widen the range of teaching and learning opportunities available to their students via such means as distance learning, student-centred learning, provision of novel (not necessarily IT-based) learning resources, and the like.

Many universities, Loughborough among them, secured funding from the FCP programme and thus initiated a range of projects covering many subjects in undergraduate and postgraduate education. There has never been any doubt that this programme included in its aims the facilitation of high quality teaching and learning experiences for much larger numbers of students, while restraining growth in staff numbers. In practice, it was also seen as a golden opportunity to broaden teaching styles and resources in a way that many undergraduate students would expect: irrespective of their numbers, we cannot hope any longer to satisfy 18+ and more mature students by a basic mix of formal lectures, tutorials and laboratory or workshop classes. It was immediately clear at Loughborough that the programme also brought into the realms of possible everyday use many novel teaching ideas previously dormant – our main problem was holding at bay the large numbers of staff who wanted to participate in our Flexible Learning Initiative (FLI) but who could not at once be accommodated despite increased University financial support!

A major aim of the FCP programme from the outset was that outcomes from individual HEIs should be as widely disseminated as possible. Loughborough University has been given responsibility for this coordinating role and the Flexible Learning Initiative team have taken on this task also. The enthusiasm and success of those running FCP programmes in many universities have been remarkable. There are clear links between the FCP programme and the (larger) IT-based Teaching and Learning Technology Programme and here also Loughborough is active, both in its own TLTP work (conducted jointly with Leicester and De Montfort University and the Open University) and in establishing means whereby TLTP outcomes can be disseminated to all HEIs. There is every indication that both these programmes will have positive results out of all proportion to their relatively modest resources and I certainly expect that the Loughborough Flexible Learning Initiative and analogous operations at other universities will become permanent and invaluable features of higher education, critical to our success as student numbers increase further and as access to HEIs is widened.

The present volume is based entirely on initiatives taken here at Loughborough under the auspices of the FLI team. Much of the work in individual academic departments has been undertaken *in addition* to the normal teaching, research and consultancy loads of the staff – another demonstration, if another were needed, of the seemingly limitless commitment of university teachers to their profession – and the range of subjects and teaching and learning approaches is truly impressive. Few of us would have guessed when the initiative began less than two years ago that we would move so far and so fast: the book is thus a tribute to the innovative hard work of its editors and contributors, who are much to be congratulated and thanked.

Jim Miller
Senior Pro-Vice-Chancellor
Loughborough University of Technology

Introduction

Winnie Wade

More means worse?

Institutions of higher education are being affected by considerable changes. Student numbers have risen dramatically since 1991 and the composition of the student population has also altered considerably. More mature and part-time students are now entering higher education and the proportion of students with non-standard entry qualifications has increased. There is greater pressure on teaching accommodation and teaching resources are in short supply as a consequence of changes in student-staff ratios. Staff are now being faced with increased assessment loads. The maintenance of quality is becoming a priority in educational institutions and consequently quality audit and assessment systems are being established.

These changes present the system with a significant challenge. How is the quality of teaching to be maintained and enhanced while student numbers increase, at a reduced unit cost? How well are academic staff equipped to cope with a diversifying student population and how is the quality of student experience to be maintained? One response which meets the challenge is a flexible approach to teaching and learning which encourages flexibility at all stages, from the design of courses through to forms of assessment.

What is flexible learning?

A broad description of flexible learning is that it is an approach to university education which provides students with the opportunity to take greater responsibility for their learning and to be engaged in learning activities and opportunities that meet their own individual needs. Tomlinson and Kilner (1991) argue that flexible learning emphasizes adaptation to the varying learning needs of students and the promotion of their learning autonomy, within a framework of appropriate support.

Beyond that, however, flexible learning as a concept can have many different meanings to different individuals. The terms open learning, distance learning and flexible learning are often used synonymously.

Open learning is a term used to describe courses flexibly designed to meet individual requirements. Lewis and Spencer (1986) explain that 'it is often applied to provision which tries to remove barriers that prevent attendance at more traditional courses but it also suggests a philosophy'.

Distance learning, although possessing similar characteristics, implies geographical distance between the learner and the providing institution.

Usually the learning occurs with the aid of self-study packaged materials which may include video tapes or computer software.

CSUP (1992) has claimed that the broad term flexible learning has been used as a banner under which to promote a shift from formal, whole-class didactic teaching towards individual or group management of learning. This is achieved through the provision by the tutor of structured resource materials together with opportunities for the negotiation of tasks, self- and peer-assessment and collaborative group work. Although labelling the approach 'flexible learning' helps to bring out the logical priority of learning and the goal of student autonomy, the approach is clearly concerned with assisting that learning and promoting that autonomy. The development of any form of flexible learning therefore requires a strong framework of support and guidance for the student from the outset. This support cannot just be provided by the tutor but must be part of an institutional support structure which provides for the student's learning needs. The flexible learning framework (TVEI, 1991) lists as a main institutional implication that clear and easily accessed learner support frameworks must be in place to provide appropriate support for students to take on increased responsibility.

Flexibility in course provision in higher education

Flexible delivery methods are an attractive option when seeking to improve the effectiveness and quality of teaching in higher education. Considerable investment of time and money is, however, required for such innovations on a large scale.

In 1992 the former Universities Funding Council initiated a programme to encourage flexibility in course provision. The purpose of this programme was to promote the development of more flexible patterns of teaching and learning and a review of the content and structure of courses. Support was provided for 28 varied projects at 22 higher education institutions under the Flexibility in Course Provision (FCP) programme. One of these projects, the Flexible Learning Initiative, is based at Loughborough University of Technology.

The Flexible Learning Initiative

The Flexible Learning Initiative was established at Loughborough University of Technology in September 1992 in order to provide a strategic approach to the implementation of more flexible patterns of teaching and learning. Loughborough University, through the Flexible Learning Initiative, is committed to providing an environment which facilitates student involvement in the learning process and encourages students to take more responsibility for this process. A number of projects were set up within the Initiative across a range of academic departments, developing a wide variety of flexible learning strategies. As a result of these projects, a wider range of learning opportunities has been provided for the students, with a broader repertoire of teaching strategies in use by staff.

Flexible learning issues

A number of important questions need to be considered when embedding flexible learning within the teaching programmes of an institution of higher education. The benefits of introducing innovative teaching methods must be weighed against the costs. Benefits include the improvement of access to the courses, the shift from passive to active learning, more cost-effective use of space and time, and the ability to interact with larger numbers of students and to support a more diverse student population.

In terms of the costs, initial investment in flexible learning approaches is high. These high costs are shown in the time it takes to set up new support structures. Of course, in relation to distance education, capital investment in teaching and residential buildings is lower than on-site teaching and assessment (CSUP, 1992). But the costs of computer-based learning can be extremely high. These costs include the purchase and installation of hardware and software and the time invested in courseware development. Costs of maintenance of equipment must be taken into account and training costs for academic staff are an important factor in the cost-benefit equation. CSUP gives a useful review of the benefits and costs of computer-based learning. In any change towards a flexible learning methodology, benefits are often long-term, and a good deal of time and effort is needed 'up-front' in order to ensure the change is successful and of benefit to the students.

Institutions need to make a major commitment to ensure that flexible learning is embedded in their structures. Any innovation in education depends to a large degree on those within an institution whose main rôle it is to support and to enable. However, a significant amount of institutional support is needed during implementation of flexible learning. The institution itself must be flexible enough to respond to change. Institutions need to develop strategic plans to address their changing rôle in the provision of innovative teaching methods and supply of appropriate resources and support. Developments in innovative methods of teaching, the support of self-paced learning, and the opportunities which educational technology presents, have major implications for the formation of policies for the development of higher education at all levels. It is significant that at Loughborough University support from senior staff has been strong right from the early stages, and real progress has been made in a relatively short time.

Another key issue is the question of management of such change within an institution. Whether the initial change is small scale or part of a whole institutional strategy, it will challenge assumptions and practices that may have been in place for some considerable time. The process of change cannot be rushed as staff may take time to adjust to new ideas. Attitudes may have to be changed and the development of new skills and competences must take place if changes in teaching and learning are to be successfully implemented. An effective programme of staff development must be provided and training must be tailored to address specific needs. A structured programme of staff training should be provided which nevertheless incorporates some flexibility to allow response to new situations. A key element of the Flexible Learning Initiative at Loughborough University was the provision of appropriately focused staff development to support changes in teaching methods.

The contents of this book

The aim of this book is to address some broad issues related to flexible learning in higher education, and to provide some specific examples of how one institution of higher education is implementing more flexible patterns of teaching and learning. The book brings together the collective experiences of staff from a variety of departments and subject areas and examines some issues, both conceptual and practical, in relation to flexible learning.

Part 1 explores broad issues related to flexible learning. It begins with a discussion of the diverse student population entering higher education today and the ways in which flexible responses can be made to student diversity and how individual needs can be met. Structural changes in degree courses have made a significant impact on teaching and learning methods and the effect of modularization and semesterization on flexible learning is examined in Chapter 2.

One important factor in considering the introduction of flexible methods is the availability of new technologies. The rapid development of learning technologies is one of the driving forces of innovation in higher education institutions. Brande (1993) has described a number of applications of computer-based technologies which include the production of learning materials, storage and rapid retrieval of information through videodiscs or databases, computer-dedicated information services such as electronic mail and computer conferences, and computer-based training programmes. The establishment of the Computers in Teaching Initiative (CTI) centres and the launch of the Teaching and Learning Technology Programme (TLTP) have great potential to influence the development of new methods of learning. The overall aim of the TLTP programme is to make teaching and learning more productive and efficient by harnessing modern technology. Successful applications and use of new technologies to develop flexible learning depend on the provision of effective support for the learner. Only too frequently are new projects limited by a failure to address pedagogic aspects. Chapter 3 shows how far the next generation of students will already have progressed in their IT skills before entry. It suggests that much careful evaluation will be needed to discover how best to integrate technology into teaching and learning and considers some ways in which information technology can play a part in students' learning.

Chapter 4 takes provision for part-time and mature students as its focus and examines how off-site flexible learners can be best supported in their studies. Practical assistance to course tutors is offered in Chapter 5 on the design of flexible course guides. It suggests that more thought, time and energy need to be invested in the presentation of learning material as one aspect of changing pedagogy.

Finally in this section, Chapter 6 explores in depth the changes which must inevitably take place in libraries so that they are able to respond effectively to flexible learning approaches. A number of issues are raised including provision of, and accommodation for, supporting resources and availability of space for students to work in groups.

Part 2 of the book takes a very practical view by examining flexible learning in action in a range of university departments. A series of examples of flexible learning are offered to readers as a resource for those wishing to change the teaching and learning methods on their courses. The chapters included in this section have been written by academic staff who are interested in change. They explore the difficulties and uncertainties which they have experienced in the development of new approaches to teaching and learning. A more detailed introduction to these case studies is given at the beginning of Part 2.

Finally, Part 3 of the book gives an insight into the student view of flexible learning. In a research project related to the departmental initiatives, samples of students were invited to discuss their reactions to innovation against a background of more traditional teaching. Their views indicate an increasingly important role for open discussion on the needs and nature of student populations, and suggest a need for a new and essentially collaborative relationship between teachers and taught.

This book is intended for all those who are concerned with innovation and good practice in teaching and learning in higher education. Key issues in relation to flexible learning have been raised. It is hoped that the strategies and examples that have been discussed will stimulate others to rethink their own teaching and adopt a more flexible approach. The benefits for students are many, not least in terms of their individual development as learners. The challenges facing higher education today must be met and flexible learning is surely a significant way forward.

References

Brande, Lieve van den (1993) *Flexible and distance learning,* Chichester: John Wiley.

The Committee of Scottish University Principals (CSUP) (1992) *Teaching and Learning in an Expanding Higher Education System. Report of a working party of CSUP,* Edinburgh: CSUP.

Lewis, R and Spencer, D (1986) *What is Open Learning?,* London: Council for Educational Technology.

Tomlinson, P and Kilner, S (1991) *Flexible Learning, Flexible Teaching: The flexible learning framework and current educational theory,* Sheffield: Employment Department.

Technical and Vocational Educational Initiative (TVEI) (1991) *Flexible Learning: A framework for education and training in the skills decade,* Sheffield: Employment Department.

Part One: Broad Issues in Flexible Learning

Chapter One

Flexible Provision for Student Diversity

Keith Hodgkinson

Expansion and diversity

In planning to expand higher education provision in the 1990s the government clearly intended to widen access to non-traditional groups. As a consequence, 'Not only will entry requirements and procedures have to be changed; institutions of higher education will have to adapt their teaching methods and the design of their courses to accommodate new types of student' (DES, 1987).

If by 'traditional students' is meant a homogeneous group aged 18–21, white, British, middle-class and 'hardly ever ugly' (Tight, 1988), then the characteristic of non-standard students is the extent of their heterogeneity. They come in all shapes and sizes, with or without formal qualifications, at any age and in very individual personal and economic circumstances. Localized research indicates considerable differences in patterns of recruitment between institutions even within the same geographical region. Intake figures vary partly as a reflection of different application, admissions and recording practices, and partly by academic subject strengths. Total numbers of non-standard students are rarely high (MacDonald, 1992) except for those institutions such as the Open University and Birkbeck College, London, which specialize in non-standard provision. Elsewhere the one reasonably common trend would seem to be the increase in the pressure for vocational academic courses from women returnees (Hart, 1988). Moreover, one of the effects of increasingly mixed modes of provision in higher education has been the blurring of the once-clear distinction between full- and part-time modes of study, between the mature student and the school leaver, between European and domestic students.

Policy and action

By the essentially egalitarian terms of their charters, universities and colleges have always been reluctant to make discriminatory policy in favour of what are seen as minority groups. The furthest that institutions are normally prepared to go is to develop equal opportunity clauses in line with statements of support for non-standard students. Historically there has been a gradual and steady translation of generalized public policy by even the most traditional of Higher Education institutions. Separate teaching or welfare units have been set up to cover specific needs on demand. Such support mechanisms have sometimes been under-recognized and under-financed but their committees rarely ask for cost-benefit accounting. Often the institution is very aware that gains are made in PR terms. In sum, there has been a localized, flexible and increasingly regularized and more appropriately funded response in recent years.

It is debatable whether such a development indicates 'a genuine desire to open up higher educational opportunities to mature students and others from non-traditional backgrounds', or 'an expedient means to compensate for demographic changes which have cut back on institutions' traditional intakes' (Tight, 1988). In traditional institutions, such flexibility as has been developed is therefore usually a product of individual or departmental initiative often in the face of political pressures to, for instance, increase admission points or improve quality through efficiency.

Diversity by locality and degree subject makes an appropriate response less likely at the institutional level. In the absence of well-founded national statistics there is clearly a great danger of ad hoc reactions to individual student needs by individual course tutors. The proactive design of flexible courses for student diversity needs to be related to global trends in order to anticipate and respond to further demand.

Flexibility for diversity

There are a number of general points to be made about flexible responses to student diversity. First, regulations can be modified to allow for a higher proportion of wider access students as in the English Access and the Scottish Wider Access and Mature Student Entry programmes. Induction can be smoothed by the development of pre-course study skills teaching and, for overseas groups, language and cultural adjustment programmes. For students on courses requiring linear learning, such as maths, physics, chemistry and languages, the prerequisite for a standard level of 'hard' knowledge can be met by specific 'Return to study' courses. Mid-course modules may also need to be preceded by similar units plus appropriate counselling.

Flexibility should thus extend well beyond technical matters of qualification and intellectual suitability. Academic success will very much depend on the meeting of other needs, whether social, dietary, spiritual or domestic. Much depends on students' linguistic and cultural background, learning skills and methods of study experience, and the meeting of sometimes very personal needs, eg family settlement, needs of children in schools and the process of cultural adjustment. For non-standard students the notion of course or study flexibility will present problems in terms of their expectations and of their perception of standards and legitimacy (Weil, 1986). Students from socially and politically repressive regimes, for example, may approach loosely structured and non-authoritarian study practices very differently from those from more liberal backgrounds.

Generic information retrieval and investigation skills need to be taught by student support and library services. For this, entry skills for information work need to be identified and more advanced information skills should be offered before major project and research activity. More specific library skills programmes should be keyed into departmental requirements and made available on demand for non-standard groups or designed as flexible self-teaching units.

Flexible course design will only meet the needs of non-standard students when strong support mechanisms, the infrastructure of diversity, are in place.

Mature students

Financial considerations will colour the interest of mature students in traditional courses since their grant-earning capacity as fully independent students is frequently more than offset by the need to meet accumulated commitments. In a recession, redundancy and early retirement create a buoyant market for higher education but students seeking a second career may compete only for places on vocational courses with a strong employment payoff. For those without sufficient support, part-time courses are a particularly attractive option. Thus the distinction between mature and part-time groups is easily blurred and so for our purposes the two groups will be considered together. The particular needs of mature students are discussed further in Chapter 4.

Part-time students

Those part-time and mature students who have experienced twilight, home or worked-based learning programmes will already be familiar with many features of flexible learning and will have well-developed time management skills. Their experience could be exploited by encouraging them to share with traditional students who will be less secure in flexible environments. On the other hand some may prefer more tightly structured courses in order to maximize their limited time and opportunities for learning. They may find the traditional lecture/seminar format more stimulating and more efficient for their needs. Their right to opt out of as well as in to flexible learning schedules must be acknowledged.

Much flexibility can be built into the timing of course modules using Summer School, weekend and twilight teaching. Flexibility is needed in access to tutors and to tutorials since part-time students may or may not want twilight teaching. Similarly, provision of study facilities for 'day' students needs to be widened. Library and computing services need to be flexible, with generous opening hours more sensitive to student demand and a flexible range of loan periods.

Technical developments, though initially very expensive, would open up more versatile study practices. Lap-top word processors, e-mail links and international computer networking will allow part-timers to continue to study in the home and in the workplace. Teleconferencing would encourage tutors to design courses around group and syndicated learning and would reduce problems of tutor-student access. Off-site library access will enhance study patterns and will help to level out the differences between residential and off-site activity.

Finally, it is important to recognize that part-timers may either be in work or out of work. The former have transferable skills and experience to be recognized. Both sub-groups need prior learning and achievement to be recognized via credit transfer.

Disabled students

A generation of disabled students has now benefited from support from specifically appointed tutors and units within Higher Education institutions. Unfortunately, statistics on the pattern of disabled student participation in higher education are not very meaningful, relying, as they do, on self-disclosure on the UCAS application form. The government collects and publishes only figures on the registered disabled, which can be very misleading in terms of actual student needs. Carefully worded institutional literature has encouraged applicants to volunteer information on needs such as epilepsy and dyslexia which they might otherwise fear to admit. Discussion with administrators and responsible tutors has provided the author with anecdotal evidence that, in fact, something like 2 to 5 per cent of students currently request support on arrival.

In a sense, an appropriate response to an individual student need represents a flexible learning initiative. Traditionally-taught courses present disabled students with many fairly obvious physical barriers to learning (Griffiths *et al.*, 1993). Any study programme dependent on core lectures in traditional lecture theatres will present specific problems. These include for example:

● wheelchair access and participation
● deafness
  – with or without an induction loop system
  – lip reading of a moving lecturer

- blindness/partially sighted
  - OHP/board clarity (especially in maths)
- dyslexia
  - note-making (see Aspden and Hinton, 1993).

Many difficulties could be removed or reduced by technical and therefore expensive modifications to the lecturing environment, such as ramps and lifts, modified doorways, space clearance at the front or centre, tape recording and pre-lecture recording or handouts. The primary source of such information is to be found in Part M of the current Building Regulations (Department of the Environment, 1992) which cover all new buildings and major rebuilding projects. Older structures present more serious problems and may require professional advice and discussion with individual students. The attendance of a British Sign Language interpreter provides satisfactory communication at all venues except, possibly, for open discussion groups. Pre-lecture communication between interpreter and tutor should avoid frantic finger-spelling (slower than BSL) of unexpected technical terminology. Visually impaired students now have access to larger print through more sophisticated copying, and Braille now extends to tactile diagrams of various types (Hinton, 1993). Course guides and flexible learning packs should be available in such modified forms.

In many respects the move towards flexible learning creates enormous advantages for disabled students. They have more to gain than most people from information technology. Adapted terminals in each teaching room are still needed, but a well-resourced residential room will include adapted networking and e-mail facilities as well as personal access to library and other information sources. Peer discussion and collaborative work may be organized in such accommodation. Self-paced study releases those with particular medical needs from their dependence on fixed lecture timings, as exemplified by a mathematical sciences student in Chapter 9.

The final point is that for all of these provisions the real expert is the disabled student. It is all too easy for well-intentioned and even experienced providers to embark on their own solutions without consulting the individual student who is to receive 'benefit'. The student must be involved in the planning and be empowered to influence the decisions of professional advisers, yet not be made to feel the weight of responsibility for future learning. There is a fine balance to be struck between overzealous and overbearing provision, however sensitive and 'flexible', and responsive and supportive enablement.

Overseas students

Types of student need and social expectation will vary enormously. The study requirements of most courses create general linguistic and social barriers, but these needs cannot be considered or dealt with *en bloc*. Apart from specific language backgrounds, there are many pitfalls for the unwary tutor. For example, North American, EC and ex-Commonwealth/Pakistan students do not necessarily speak English or have experience of Roman script. Those from authoritarian or very traditional (and sometimes formerly British colonial) educational backgrounds may need induction into western-European learning processes. The concept of open libraries, where literature is available on open shelves without ordering and there is unrestricted access to information, may come as a considerable culture shock. Some cultures do not accord equal status to female staff and some have a very keen awareness of the significance of professional and academic hierarchy. A period of disorientation will precede acclimatization and acculturation.

Many overseas students will therefore require strong personal and academic support before starting their courses. Departmental personal tutoring systems should prepare for problems of isolation and identity crisis which can be worsened by the lack of a compulsory structure at the centre of a course. The provision of specialist teaching to individuals and necessarily small groups across the campus makes the establishment of a properly funded support structure a matter of central planning and provision. Language support units struggle to gain academic recognition while they are insecurely staffed and find research work inappropriate. Study skills programmes need to be carefully designed to take account of individual differences, especially where information retrieval and manipulation are concerned. Library staff need to interact with other service groups.

Overseas students may not have encountered many flexible learning techniques. They may be unused to open discussion with tutors or even with their peers. The notion of peer discussion, student-led tutorials/seminars, conferencing, syndicated study groups and team assessment may be anathema to students, as indicative of lower standards. Their performance, initially, may be held back if study modes require mature social interaction and well-developed social skills. Initiative may have to be explained and fostered. On the other hand many may well be very experienced in individualized work.

The future?

Market forces alone may not be enough to encourage universities to develop increasingly diverse patterns of teaching and study opportunities. In the next few years increasingly diverse student populations, constraints on student funding and the subsequent development of loans may well lead many more undergraduates to look to their local university for their first and higher degrees. A rise in residential costs and the consequent reduction in the number of campus-based students will increase the pressure to provide a wider and more flexible base of study facilities and to open up teaching hours within a standard week and academic year. On- and off-site movement and learning links will destroy the traditional isolationism of the campus and of restricted notions of academic values.

Improved information technology will undoubtedly increase the versatility of learning patterns especially for non-standard student groups. Inter-regional and international links at cheap telephone rates (via fibre-optic technology) will make the unitary residential campus pattern look increasingly obsolete. Distance packages may replace all direct face-to-face and group teaching as tutors increasingly look to wider reference groups and build teleconferencing, based on campus, into all course tutoring (Searle, 1993). More flexible patterns of peer contact – between part- and full-timers, between mature, off-site and residential individuals, between home and overseas groups and between different cohorts of the latter – could revolutionize the individualized nature of traditional learning in higher education. Wider access, flexible accreditation and course structure, and personal computer use may be only the beginning of the development of a pattern of truly open learning in higher education, with an open campus operating (nearly) all hours and with opt-in teaching patterns to meet the increasingly varied needs of all types of student.

Acknowledgements

In preparing this chapter the author gratefully acknowledges the help of the following staff at Loughborough University: Dr Ron Hinton (Senior Tutor for Students with Special Needs), Janet Stevenson (Language Support Unit), Peter Lewis (Maths Department), Mary Hodgkinson (Library) and Jim White (Student Records).

References

Aspden, S and Hinton, R (1993) 'Dyslexia and the university student', in *Working with Students with Special Needs: A Compendium Volume*, Sheffield: CVCP Universities Staff Development Unit.

Department of the Environment (1992) *Building Regulations 1991, Approved Document M: Access and Facilities for Disabled People*, London: HMSO.

DES (1987) *Higher Education: Meeting the challenge*, Cm. 114, London: HMSO.

Griffiths, S, Hinton, R and Wilson, A (1993) *Working with Students with Special Needs*, Sheffield: Universities Staff Development Unit of the Committee of Vice-Chancellors and Principals.

Hart, L (1988) *Women's Perceived Education and Training Needs*, Leicester: NIACE.

Hinton, R (1993) 'Tactile and audio-tactile images as vehicles for learning', in Burger, D and Sperandio, J-C, *Non-visual Human-computer Interactions: Prospects for the visually handicapped*, pp. 169–79, Paris: Inserm, John Libby Eurotext.

MacDonald, I (1992) 'Meeting the needs of non-traditional students: challenge or opportunity for higher education', *Scottish Journal of Adult Education*, 1, 2, 34–46.

Searle, M (1993) 'Campus without walls', *Times Higher Education Supplement*, 19 November.

Tight, M (1988) 'The practical implications of non-standard provision', *Teaching News*, 34, June, pp. 3–4.

Weil, S W (1986) 'Non-traditional learners within traditional higher education institutions: discovery and disappointment', *Studies in Higher Education*, 11, 3, 219–35.

Chapter Two

Flexibility in Course Structures

John Costello

Degree courses in universities

The second half of the twentieth century can be presented as a time of considerable growth in university education in Britain. Many new universities have been built, and many other institutions have become universities. Despite this development and diversity, however, the dominant style of undergraduate courses has not changed. The majority of university students follow a three-year honours degree programme in a named academic subject. For these students, flexibility in course provision is of little significance.

It is tempting to argue that the specialized three-year honours degree is demonstrably robust, because of its survival and dominance over many years. It has stood the test of time. But the test is an artificial one. Full-time degree courses of this kind have been supported favourably. Fees are paid by local education authorities on a mandatory basis. In most cases, these fees are supplemented substantially through central government funding councils. Furthermore, students are entitled to apply for maintenance grants and, although these are means-tested and are being replaced partially by a loan system, these grants continue to be of help to large numbers of less-affluent students. For other forms of higher education, financial support from public funds is discretionary – which generally means unavailable.

The effect of earmarked funding for a particular type of higher education is, of course, to distort the market. Course provision is governed not by popular demand but by the providers, who are able to offer free tuition and access to grants for courses which they choose to provide. While it is the universities that make this choice, their freedom is inevitably restricted by government funding policies.

The narrowly specified allocation of public support has a discriminatory function. It means that those who have the ability, motivation and background to follow a specialized, full-time degree course are given a large advantage over their peers. The rhetoric about free access to higher education means free access for a chosen minority.

Mass access to higher education is an enormously expensive investment. Any government which chooses to subsidize students must make decisions about the students and courses which it supports, so that some form of discrimination is inevitable. Comparisons are commonly made between Britain and the United States: the popular view is that access to American universities is probably less dependent on high academic ability than in Britain but more dependent on financial factors. This is a misleading over-simplification. Thody (1993) points to the large difference in fees between, for example, Stanford and Berkeley Universities, and to the effect this has on the ethnic mix of students. The clear difference between American and British practice, however, is in the amount of specialization: at Stanford, at most two-thirds of the work for a degree can be within one major discipline. This is in stark contrast to the British system of named subject qualifications, which more often seeks to restrict the proportion which can be taken *outside* the major subject.

These examples, like many others often quoted, are from California. Indeed, the more flexible and less specialized pattern of degree courses prevalent in the United States is sometimes described as the 'Californian model' (Reed, 1991). It appears, however, that elective systems of modular courses and credit accumulation were pioneered at Harvard and over the years have become the standard pattern in American universities (Davidson, 1992). In Britain in the 1990s, universities are experiencing both internal and external pressures for change. Modularization, semesterization and credit accumulation are fashionable ideas and these lead, by implication, to a new consideration of timetabling and of the classification of degree awards. There are three important external factors, too. First, many former polytechnics and colleges of higher education have become universities, creating a much larger and more diverse sector. Second, in a relatively short time there has been a substantial, under-funded expansion of undergraduate student numbers. Third, the automatic entitlement to fees and other financial benefits for full-time degree students is no longer sacrosanct. All these pressures force universities to reconsider their pattern of provision. The era of specialist full-time degrees has been something of an ice age in British higher education. Perhaps we are now seeing the thaw.

Flexibility through semesterization

The Flowers Committee (HEFCE, 1993) recommended the restructuring of the academic year on a semester basis. This recommendation recognized a development which was already agreed in principle by many universities, and in some cases partially implemented.

For many years, the normal pattern of undergraduate courses in universities required about 30 weeks attendance in each academic year, divided into three ten-week terms. Since most degree programmes were provided by specialist subject departments, it was the responsibility of departments to organize the teaching and the timetable within those three terms.

Assessment commonly included a number of formal, written examinations, held in the later part of the Summer term. Given time for revision and marking, this pattern has usually implied perhaps 24 or 25 weeks of teaching in each year. So long as courses were largely the responsibility of individual departments, the traditional academic year worked reasonably well. The department could decide how to divide up and timetable the course, and how best to use the relatively short teaching period in the Summer term. However, when courses are broken up into smaller units or modules, when more options are made available to students outside their main department, and particularly when courses shorter than the full academic year are included in the programme, problems begin to arise.

If a course is taught entirely in the Autumn term, it is unsatisfactory to postpone its assessment until the following Summer. A written examination, delayed for six months, is obviously unattractive. But, whether or not there is a formal examination, it is usually considered better to provide students with more immediate feedback on their performance.

Another difficulty in the three-term system is the effective use of time. A subject department which provides the bulk of a degree programme may have no difficulty in planning 24 or 25 weeks of teaching. But if a range of shorter courses are offered as contributions to various programmes, it is more natural and convenient to provide these on a one-term basis. In some cases, where degrees include a substantial number of elective modules from several departments, this has led to a concentration of work in the Autumn and Spring, and a gradual erosion of teaching in the Summer term.

These are some of the considerations which have led to a division of the academic year into two 15-week semesters. There has been some suspicion that this is the prelude to the introduction of a third 15-week semester, allowing for a box-and-cox system with each student attending for two of the three semesters, or possibly for accelerated, two-year degree programmes in some cases. These suspicions are fuelled by political demands for more intensive use of plant. At the time of writing, however, financial constraints make the expansion implied by a third semester unlikely. It remains, perhaps, an option for the future, particularly if a greater proportion of the cost of higher education is paid by students themselves.

The division of the academic year into two semesters for teaching purposes, with assessment at the end of each semester, does not necessarily imply changing the dates of terms and vacations. It is quite possible to impose semesters on existing terms. Twelve weeks can be timetabled for teaching (broken by a lengthy Christmas vacation) followed by a three-week assessment period. After this a further 12-week teaching block can begin more or less immediately, leaving the last three weeks of the year for assessment of the second block. There are some perceived disadvantages in this, but it is clear that, even before the Flowers recommendations were published, a number of universities had taken a decision to implement a system of this kind, regardless of the dates of terms.

A survey by Davidson (1992) of the sizes of standard course units, suggests that a pattern of 12 weeks teaching followed by three weeks for assessment will become normal practice in the 1990s. It is clear that in some programmes, some subject departments will continue to extol the value of longer units of study and teaching, operating throughout the academic year and assessed at the end of the year. For this reason, it is unlikely that all course units will be confined to 12-week blocks. In some cases, the preferred model may be affected more by personal and historical factors than by the demands of a particular academic subject. Nevertheless, there is some indication that humanities subjects may require more year-long units, while mathematics and pure science specialists are more likely to be content with courses taught in 12-week blocks. These concerns have led some universities to consider the possibility of two semesters of unequal length, perhaps 14 and 16 weeks respectively, each with 12 teaching weeks but with the greater part of the assessment at the end of the academic year.

As a result of the Flowers report, it seems likely that most universities will now abandon the three-term structure and move to a full semester system. The preferred pattern is for 15 weeks before Christmas and 15 after. There are difficulties with this. It means starting the year at the very beginning of September. For the first-year intake, this has implications for the processing of admissions, which depends in turn on the timing of the publication of GCE A level results. This is not an insuperable problem, but it may result, initially at least, in a delayed start for first-year students.

Flexibility through modularization

Modularization usually refers to the division of each year of a degree course into smaller discrete units of a standard size. The system introduced at Loughborough University of Technology in 1991, for example, required full-time students to complete 12 modules in each year. Like other systems, this structure allowed for double modules and in some cases for triple and larger modules, but the notional division of the student's work load in each year into 12 parts was clear. Each module could be taught entirely within one term or could operate throughout the year on a 'long, thin' basis.

Modularization in this sense is an enabling device which can be used to promote a number of developments. It provides an institutional basis on which to review the comparability of demands made by different degree programmes, and to devolve funding in an equitable way to departments responsible for different aspects of teaching. It can lead to more efficient teaching where one module is seen as an appropriate part of several different programmes. It can increase student choice where degree programmes include a number of optional or elective modules. If general regulations are expressed in terms of modules, course and programme regulations are much simplified. They can consist simply of a menu of compulsory and optional modules in each year. Finally, modularization can be a step towards the development of course provision which is more flexible in a number of ways.

Comparability between different degree programmes is always difficult. The division of a year's work into smaller, manageable units can help to quantify the student's work load. It is possible to define what is a reasonable range of staff-student contact time for each module, and even the approximate study time which one module requires. Close monitoring of student work is thus more manageable and more accurate. Such a definition must allow for some flexibility: the appropriate balance of timetabled sessions and individual study in particular may vary considerably between different subject areas and different groups of students.

A separate issue, which is nevertheless related to work load, is the devolution of funding to departments responsible for teaching. Here, an obvious model is to allocate a fixed amount of funding per student-module. This allows academic staff to take professional decisions about the number of hours of teaching each module requires. Such a system can obviously be tuned more finely in various ways. It seems appropriate to recognize teaching in parallel with the recognition of research, but it is not appropriate to reward departments which give students excessively heavy timetables.

There are plenty of opportunities in a modular structure for making teaching more efficient. Closely similar modules in different degree programmes may be identified. Some may question the effectiveness of teaching very large groups, but large numbers of relatively small groups of students taking modules in, say, statistics or information technology, can prove costly and inefficient. While the effectiveness in terms of learning, and of cost, of course provision are sometimes in conflict, both are valid criteria for planning. Unfortunately, there are other, less helpful considerations: one which gives rise to concern is departmental protectiveness towards students.

When named subject departments are responsible for recruiting students and for arranging appropriate programmes for them, it is reasonable that those departments should take a proprietary interest in their students. This, however, can encourage a policy of teaching as much of the programme as possible within the parent department. Moreover, formula funding based on student-modules may be a further incentive for this form of ring-fencing. These same attitudes can lead to reduced flexibility and a more restricted range of choices for students.

The restructuring of undergraduate courses in modular form at Loughborough University of Technology produced a number of benefits. It had some success in providing a logical allocation of teaching-related funding to departments, in addressing issues of comparability of work load, in encouraging more efficient teaching and, to some extent, in increasing the range of options available to students. Since, however, the modular structure was applied directly to the existing system of named, single and joint honours degrees, it had very limited capacity to promote more flexible innovation in course provision. In order to allow further development, while preserving the advantages of modularization, a decision has now been taken to introduce a system of credit accumulation at undergraduate level.

Flexible credit accumulation

Credit accumulation schemes allow students to build up 'credit' towards a degree, by completing courses each of which carries a certain 'credit weighting'. Most commonly in Britain, a year's full-time study is imagined as carrying 120 credits, so that a BA or BSc degree is awarded on the basis of 360 credits.

Within a credit accumulation scheme, the modules can vary in size. Like modularization, credit accumulation can be imposed on an existing system of named degree courses made up of prescribed components, and indeed such courses are likely to remain the norm for some time. But credit accumulation becomes useful and interesting when students are allowed to negotiate and construct their own degree programme, with a range of subject content and a time-scale which suit their individual needs.

The so-called 'old' universities are latecomers to modular and credit accumulation schemes. A number of former polytechnics and, of course, the Open University have operated such systems successfully for a number of years. At postgraduate level, however, some universities have a tradition of offering masters degrees by 'negotiated studies', allowing students to use whatever courses were appropriate to construct a suitable postgraduate programme. At this level, the introduction of a credit accumulation scheme has proved relatively straightforward: a masters degree can be obtained on the basis of postgraduate modules amounting to, say, 120 credits, of which 40 might normally be derived from a dissertation.

Inevitably, the great majority of taught masters degree students continue to follow established programmes in specific academic disciplines. Again, this is to some extent governed by financial considerations: available bursaries and grants are often allocated to particular subject areas. But, even when funding is not a consideration, there appears to be little demand for broadly-based combined studies programmes at postgraduate level. Indeed, most candidates are looking for a relatively minor variation on an existing subject programme.

The experience of credit accumulation at postgraduate level indicates some of the issues which will become important if such schemes become a significant part of undergraduate provision. One such issue is the erosion of the distinction between full- and part-time studies, and the related fee structure. It seems logical that fees should be charged for each module, proportional to the credit weighting of the module: it is not easy to reconcile this with the current system of annual fees. Another concern is the effect of failure in one aspect of the course. In most undergraduate courses, students who attend classes and complete the work are not disqualified by lack of success in one component of the course: there are devices for compensation and aggregation of marks to cope with this situation. For more critical failure, there is usually provision for re-examination; but repeated failure may lead to termination of studies.

There is a need for rules about the number of credits which make up a student's degree programme. There also need to be rules about levels, about the number of introductory or advanced modules and about the number derived from a single major subject which are required or permissible. Decisions have to be made about how failure in a small number of the required credits can be countenanced, compensated or redeemed. Are there any circumstances in which a student's studies should be terminated in a credit accumulation scheme? It is conceivable that students might be allowed to take any number of modules, passing some and failing others until they acquire the necessary number of credits.

One of the most intransigent aspects of moving to credit accumulation at undergraduate level, however, is the classification of honours degrees.

The classification of honours degrees

The classification of degrees on a scale ranging from first class honours to ordinary or pass degrees is a well-established characteristic of British higher education. Comparisons across institutions and across different subject areas are difficult, so that it is doubtful whether a particular class of degree has any absolute value. The classification is, however, widely used for selection purposes and its general acceptance makes institutions reluctant to change the system.

The traditional way of determining a degree classification has been by averaging marks. Some components of a degree course may be given greater weight than others and later years in particular may count for more, but basically the class of degree awarded depends on the student's average percentage mark.

It is questionable whether the traditional system of classifying degrees makes sense in a flexible credit accumulation scheme. Arguably, a transcript of a student's performance is much more useful, if this can include details of all the courses completed successfully, their credit weighting and an indication of any areas of outstanding performance. Each student accumulates credits from all modules studied and can claim a degree when the required total is achieved. It is, of course, perfectly possible to attach a percentage mark to each module and to classify the degree by an average of these marks, weighted as appropriate. But there are many who feel that this parallel but separate accounting of both credits and marks is illogical and unsatisfactory.

A number of alternative approaches are possible. For example, success in each module might be graded on a five point scale, A to E: the degree could then be classified according to the overall profile. First class honours might require at least 100 credits at grade A and at least 200 at A or B. An upper second could demand 100 at A or B and at least 200 at A, B or C; and so on. It is, however, difficult to devise such a profile which will generate a distribution of grades similar to that produced by average marks. Perhaps this is not to be expected, but it may be considered desirable.

A compromise approach is to use a grade point average for classification purposes. Grades E to A might be given points 1 to 5, and a suitable weighted average of all credits obtained can then be translated to a classification. Obviously, in such a system, classification boundaries can be set as 4.3, 3.5 or whatever, so as to create the intended distribution. This means that, within the institution, degree classification is norm-referenced rather than related to any absolute level of achievement.

Timetabling issues

In the development of flexible and innovative styles of teaching and learning, the timetable can all too easily become a constraint. It is also designed, obviously, by the provider rather than the students who use it and, however sympathetically planned, it becomes a mechanism for controlling what is possible.

Universities are large and diffuse institutions, and academic staff bring a range of attitudes and traditions to their teaching. Even at the simplest level, if a module is to have 36 hours of timetabled sessions over 12 weeks, there will be strong feelings about whether this should be in short periods spread throughout each week or in 12 three-hour blocks.

If flexibility is to mean responsiveness to student choice, so that sensible cross-curricular and interdepartmental programmes can be constructed, the various preferences of teaching staff may need to be examined and justified. The construction of a timetable, possibly involving slots of different forms for different modules, requires a subtle balancing of a range of pressures and constraints.

Structures for flexible course provision

The management of degree courses and their associated regulations is a significant factor in promoting flexible learning. Such management must involve a measure of prescriptiveness, for example about the extent to which students are prevented from or pushed into over-specialization. Part-time study can be made easier or more difficult. Strategies can be devised to encourage access; or the students can be recruited largely from traditional backgrounds. The system of accreditation of innovative courses can be responsive to change, or it can be highly conservative. Sometimes, innovation is introduced as a small annex to existing arrangements. Thus, modular courses have in some cases been developed alongside established subject courses. Access policies have been formulated which preserve almost all existing recruitment but make a few places available for non-standard applicants. Flexible learning units may enable some staff and students to work in new ways but leave large sections of the curriculum unaffected.

It is not surprising that structural change in universities is often somewhat tentative. Radical reform which threatens to thwart established and sometimes cherished practice is unlikely to succeed. On the other hand, it is unfortunate if potentially valuable developments are sidelined as fringe activities. It may be of interest to compare change in higher education with other forms of institutional innovation. Evidence summarized by Rogers (1984) indicates that in order for change to flourish it must support and affirm existing practice. The dependence is summarized simply:

Compatibility of an innovation with a preceding idea can either speed up or retard its rate of adoption. Old ideas are the main tools with which new ideas are assessed. One cannot deal with an innovation except on the basis of the familiar and the old-fashioned. Previous practice is a familiar standard against which the innovation can be interpreted, thus decreasing uncertainty.

There is perhaps a message here for those conducting research into changes in course provision in higher education. Evaluative research which identifies educational benefits is unlikely to be sufficient to promote radical development.

References

Davidson, G (1992) 'Credit accumulation and transfer and the student experience', in Barnett, R (ed.), *Learning to Effect*, Buckingham: SRHE and Open University Press.

HEFCE (1993) *The Flowers Report: The review of the academic year – A report of the committee of enquiry into the organisation of the academic year*, Bristol: HEFCE.

Reed, J (1991) 'New module army', *Oxford Magazine*, 76.

Rogers, E (1984) *Diffusion of Innovations* (3rd edn), London: Collier-Macmillan.

Thody, P (1993) 'Basking in the sun and baulking at Baudelaire', *Times Higher Education Supplement*, 24 December.

Chapter Three

Flexible Learning and Information Technology in Higher Education

Phil Wild

Introduction

Within this chapter the contribution of information technology (IT) towards flexible learning will be interpreted extremely widely. It will include the contribution to distance learning via electronic networks, open learning through student controlled learning pathways, and the process of changing teaching and learning styles by using a narrow range of IT-based facilities which fill a particular need for a particular topic within a particular course. All are valid uses of IT, and IT can also provide a medium for teaching and learning and contribute to flexibility in course provision.

What will be argued is that increasingly students will be ready for such pedagogy when they enter higher education, and that the increased hardware power and networking facilities now make the manipulation of *relevant* information possible at a level which can contribute to flexibility in teaching and learning and enhance the quality of the students' experiences. It will also be argued that it is fallacious to view most IT-based learning as part of a cost-cutting exercise, that administrators and policy makers underrate the problems and time-scale of implementing such changes, and that the 'software power' (through the user interface) is not yet at a level which makes the use of IT-based flexible learning an option for many university staff.

There are two strands which need to be considered:

- learning to use IT through flexible learning;
- using IT for flexible learning.

Both aspects have an important and growing role in students' learning.

Learning to use IT through flexible learning

There are already many developments in students learning to use IT through flexible learning. The majority of undergraduates are now able to use word-processors, and a growing number of undergraduate assignments are now in word-processed format. Few of these undergraduates will have been given any formal training with the word-processing packages. Some will use IBM PC and compatible computers, some will use Apple Macintosh, and some will use other hardware bases. The learning has been individual and based on manuals of various types, peer support and the 'ask someone who knows' process. Students now import pictures drawn by themselves using a self-taught drawing package. Obviously we are dealing with an able section of the population who are capable of fulfilling a need when the need is identified.

Evidence therefore exists from current practice that students in higher education are capable of learning to use IT through flexible learning means if the need is apparent. University computer services departments have supported this mode of learning for many years by providing 'beginners guides' to popular software packages.

Using IT for flexible learning

This mode of using IT is much more fundamental to the future direction of teaching and learning throughout the education system as a whole. As far back as the 1970s, the predictions of the future role of computers in taking over the job of the teacher were common. Both information technology and the process of teaching and learning involve the storage, retrieval and manipulation of information, so it seems natural that the former can contribute to the latter, especially as more powerful computers are able to handle the type of information relevant to the more general education arena. In 1986, as part of a crystal ball-gazing exercise on the future school curriculum, Saunders (1986) felt that 'information technology is revolutionary in that it puts learning into the hands and control of the learner'. It is worth looking at the reality of this vision, and at the contributions towards achieving it throughout the education system. To do this we need to look at:

● the experiences of students prior to higher education;
● developments in information technologies;
● teaching methodology and students' learning;
● costs and cost-effectiveness.

The experiences of students prior to higher education

There is little doubt that information technology is of growing importance within the 5–18 education sector. Throughout Britain there is an entitlement to IT for all pupils in the 5–16 (compulsory age) range due to the National Curriculum. It is expected that the programmes of study and attainment targets, which are specifically defined, should be delivered and tested within the context of a wide range of subjects. The use of IT, however, precedes the National Curriculum and its power to contribute to enhanced learning has been identified by Her Majesty's Inspectorate (HMI) based on evidence of their own surveys. In 1989 they stated that:

The nature and balance of much work within the curriculum are likely to be radically changed ... Compared with current practice there is likely to be an increasing emphasis on the quality of communication; and greater stress on high-level thinking, on interpretation and on creative expression. Especially in the later key stages, the use of technology to measure, to collate and to display the results of experiments or investigations allows increased time for, and emphasis on, analysis and interpretation. More is likely to be expected of pupils in terms of creative expression and conceptual understanding because of the reduced need to engage in or master routine techniques (DES, 1989, para. 23).

In a later report, based on observations of 1,300 lessons over the period 1988–92, HMI made further comments on the benefits of IT to the process of learning (DFE, 1992). They reported observing positive contributions to the learning process in the 5–18 age range in most areas of the curriculum.

There are many more developments in IT within this age range which will contribute to the readiness of higher education students to use IT-supported flexible learning. The government-funded CD-ROM in Schools Scheme has given a high profile to this technology as a support to more flexible learning styles. A recent survey of all secondary schools in three East Midlands local education authorities (LEAs) showed that 81 per cent have at least one CD-ROM system, usually based in the library resource area, and 95 per cent of these have a CD-ROM-based encyclopaedia. If pupils are to use such resources effectively then they will need to be trained in enhanced information retrieval and schools are starting to put such training in place. There is a growing number of reports of networked CD-ROM systems throughout schools to further encourage pupils and teachers towards more flexible approaches to the flow of information for learning (see, for example, Sivajnanam, 1993).

In some schools CD-ROM is becoming part of the much wider multimedia environment. Project Horizon for example, taking place in Hampshire in both primary and secondary phases, has involved a wide range of media linked via information technology. It has been found of pupils in one middle school that 'over a period of five weeks, their search and IT skills improved dramatically and they learned how to communicate and present information in a much more articulate way' (Sealey, 1994).

The National Council for Educational Technology (NCET) has recently been gathering together the wide-ranging evidence of the benefits of IT to learning. Some identified benefits are:

● IT enables greater imaginative understanding through increased access to information and new ways of accessing and communicating information;
● IT provides new forms and structures for representing knowledge which

will, as language does, affect that knowledge and the individual's relationship with it;

● IT enables users to ask 'What if ...?' – it gives the individual the power to take risks and make mistakes that would otherwise be costly in terms of time and/or materials;

● IT increases the opportunity for interpretation and application of data by making redundant the need for learners to process the data themselves;

● IT changes the nature of composition and authorship because the forms of composition are more numerous than they have been and because of the facility to combine original and second-hand material and integrate different media. (This issue will need particular attention in higher education. Will tutors ever again know whose work they are marking?)

● the use of IT provides opportunities to develop clear logical thinking, sequential understanding and study skills;

● IT enables the recording process to take place while it is being used, thus enhancing the learner's capacity to reflect upon, and the teacher's opportunity to intervene in, the learning (NCET, 1993).

Such perceptions and observations of the role of IT in learning, by HMI, NCET and many university-based researchers, are eminently transferable to the higher education sector, especially if we take on board an understanding of learning theory at the same time as developing IT-supported learning. Equally important, the IT experiences of the students which we will be recruiting in the near future will ensure the ability to capitalize on any expansion of teaching and learning supported by information technology. Such capitalization on students' innate ability to use IT could help to ensure that the quality in teaching and learning envisaged by the Higher Education Quality Council is realized. This is summarized in a paragraph from their checklist:

Institutions will wish to consider how different teaching strategies bring about their intended student learning objectives and enable students to take maximum responsibility for their own learning (HEQC, 1994).

No one would claim that all students will have experienced all aspects of IT use, but a basic competence will be available to build upon. The more mature returnee to education is also more likely to be IT-aware and (possibly) competent than in the past due to their experience in commerce and industry.

Developments in information technologies

The developments in schools have been possible because of the increased power of the technology available to them. In the higher education sector, there have been many developments reported by the Computers in Teaching Initiative (CTI). CTI was established in 1986 to:

● encourage the development of computer-assisted teaching and learning in UK universities;

- evaluate the educational potential of information technology at UK universities;
- promote an awareness of the potential of information technology among lecturers and students in all disciplines.

It is not possible to record here all that has been done and reported, and interested readers should refer to the CTI Support Services (CTISS) publications which should be found in all university libraries and many individual departments. These publications are a genuine resource for the enthusiastic, not so enthusiastic and even the cynical on up-to-date and relevant developments in the possible use of IT in teaching and learning in higher education.

The 'possible' is perhaps connected with the 'cynical' in that CTI pilot projects will, on the whole, be set up and run by enthusiasts, with enough funding to support the development of an idea which fits their interests. The results and progress are well reported and no doubt some readers will pick up ideas which prevent them from having to reinvent the basics; but such readers do not have the funding to support the development of the work. The other possibility is that the projects have been designed to produce totally transferable ideas and materials, which can be implemented at any other institution at no cost. A reasonable assumption is that the real situation is going to be somewhere between the two extremes.

The CTISS files provide some indication of how the hardware and software technology is influencing the potential use of IT in supporting more flexible learning styles. Garrett (1992) reported that the processing power increased 20-fold between 1986 and 1991, and that improving network technology will allow cross-linking of different makes and types of computers. The transferability of images and moving video will be possible and better user interfaces will allow more flexible use of software through the ability to switch in and out of various tasks easily and rapidly.

In the same CTISS file, Hamilton reports on the development of the Joint Academic Network (JANET) into SuperJANET (1,000 times performance increase over JANET). This will be the backbone of increased flexibility in national and international communications, allowing students greater access to a wider range of information sources in a range of formats, such as text, images and video (CTISS 11, p. 22). There is also the potential to link into the cable television infrastructure which uses optical-fibre technology like SuperJANET, providing such communication facilities directly to the homes of both students and academics. So where will the tutor have to be to lead a tutorial (Searl, 1993)?

In a similar way to the CTI projects, the Teaching and Learning Technology Programme in higher education is also widening our knowledge of the use of IT (TLTP, 1993). The projects have not been going for as long but the educational variety and technological range will contribute widely to our basic knowledge of how IT can support learning. Some of these projects are based around videodisc technology, which is the 30cm version of the CD-ROM technology, providing a very flexible learning resource. In addition, the disc can be controlled by a bar-code system which means that the user interface becomes more traditionally based around worksheets. Another advantage over CD-ROM is the greater range of data which can be stored, with 55,000 still screens of images or text or about 30 minutes of moving video, or any combination of these. Projects as diverse as experimental techniques in chemistry for undergraduates to classroom management and control for teacher training are in progress (Davis and Wright, 1993).

Software developments will always lag behind hardware, and this causes a problem in developing new systems of learning. The improved user interfaces will provide improved access to the technology for academics. However, if flexibility rather than constraint is inherent in the learning pathways, then the complexity of computer programming can be immense. Newer authoring programs are certainly improving access, but users still require a 'considerable time and effort to aquaint themselves with the more complex aspects of the package' (Davies et al., 1992). A lot of this software is used in industry for training purposes – but this encroaches on the perennial discussion on training and education. Most authoring packages were designed for industry where they are used in narrowly defined tasks. This provides flexibility of access, but constrains the learning, and in that way cannot really be considered to have a realistic future in higher education. Of course, the increased power of the hardware will eventually provide a base for very sophisticated software and the CTI programme is a good source of ongoing information. For example, in CTISS File 13 (Darby,1992), typical examples of conclusions are 'one thing is certain however, authoring systems are getting better and better', 'X is an effective tool for academics without special computing skills to produce CAL materials' and 'the learning of the software pales into insignificance beside the far greater problem of how and what to offer in the form of Computer Aided Learning'.

Teaching methodology and students' learning

So students have, to a growing extent, the background knowledge from previous work with IT. The students already show that they are able to learn relevant skills through their own learning pathways and the higher education system already has access to an ever improving technology to support more flexible learning styles. Why has the higher education system been slow in changing?

Thinking about the use of information technology in education should not primarily be about the technology, it is about the relevant flow of information. If the flow of information is too constrained then the learning experience will be a poor second to the more conventional learning methodology. We have to be sure that the technology can do what we are asking of it. To do all this we have to think about our pedagogy as a whole;

the total art and practice of teaching needs to come under scrutiny. The end of the last section highlighted the major problems in this area. We noted the lack of suitable software based on good teaching methodology which can at least equal a tutor's natural flexibility so that the resulting educational experience is not second best and painful to our professional integrity.

There is, however, much interest in developing the use of IT, which can be summarized by quoting the introduction to a paper on Authoring and Authoring systems:

Perhaps we exaggerate about the current level of interest in computer based teaching and learning (CBT/L) in higher education, but our real point is that we are on the verge of a major upsurge in CBT/L materials development and an increasing number of our colleagues are beginning to search around for guidance and leadership as they take their first steps in the process. Reacting to the twin imperatives of falling staffs and ever-increasing student numbers we are all finding CBT/L is fast becoming an attractive option. Obviously there are other reasons for the likely increase in CBT/L development, not least the enhancement and extension of student learning, but let us stick for the moment with the need to free up staff time from the more humdrum and repetitive aspects of their teaching activities. If the students can study at their own pace in front of a computer, and perhaps in their own time, then the lecturers will be that little bit more able to provide *prime-time* contact in addition to being able to engage in research (Gardner and Munroe, 1992, pp. 45–6).

Similar sentiments are reported by others working in this field, such as, 'this series of independent study materials (based on videodiscs) reduces the need for whole group teaching, releasing staff for tutorial or other work' (Davis and Wright, 1993).

It is going to be necessary to look at some models of flexible learning and models of CBT/L and try to match the two together into an educationally sound approach. Immediately we have the problem of which aspect of flexible learning and which definition of flexible learning is to be addressed. It will be useful to work on the basis that the computer will, to a large extent, be helping to manage the flow of information in response to students' needs, in which case the pedagogical issue becomes one of managing learning. Earlier work in this area by the Technical and Vocational Education Initiative (TVEI, 1991) has already developed a flexible learning framework which is described as 'a strategy to help teachers manage effective learning'. This splits the process up into three inter-linked 'managing' modes. Under each of these modes are specified the aims of the teacher and outcomes for the student. It is possible to match these to what we now know about the developing information technologies.

In managing student/teacher partnerships, IT could be used for the mutual benefit of both parties. There is no doubt that much of this is best done by talking together, as only in this way can students and teachers get to know each other to enable the rapport normally associated with good teaching. There are, however, ways of enhancing communications to the benefit of both. The use of electronic mail (e-mail) systems means that students can be sure of getting questions to a tutor and the tutor can manage his/her time in handling student questions, rather than having to cope with the continual stream of interruptions when trying to concentrate on other work. This also allows student queries to be answered remotely, from home for example through the use of modems. In this way, much of the communication between student and tutor could be at least maintained, and perhaps enhanced, without necessarily impinging on more tutor time when faced with a deteriorating staff/student ratio. If the student query needs a face-to-face discussion, then a time can be arranged via e-mail when the tutor will be available. This does, of course, assume that the tutor is able to manage the e-mail system effectively and efficiently, with a certain amount of self-discipline. It is now possible to send and receive complete documents via e-mail, and as this technology spreads, the handing in of assignments on paper might have to be reviewed, especially within the distance learning mode of flexible learning. The present technology already provides facilities for tutor-student conferencing, and the growing network infrastructure will add video to such systems.

Information technology is well suited to managing student use of resources. A look through the aims of the teacher and the outcomes for the student shows many areas of match to the current and developing technologies outlined above. It is all about finding, using, manipulating and managing information and information sources. New forms of interpersonal skills will need to be developed to use electronic communication systems to exchange information.

Managing student learning pathways is largely associated with the individualized mode of flexible learning, and again this could be considerably extended and enhanced through IT-supported systems. Indeed, IT could now contribute to all the statements under aims and outcomes as listed in TVEI (1991), and greater online access to the newer technologies will enable this to develop. Even working in teams and small groups can be supported by the presently available software and e-mail systems. The record of achievement and portfolio of work could be continually built up throughout the students' studies, and when the student is ready, the tutor (and even the external examiner at some distant institution) is given access to the work for summative accreditation.

Costs and cost-effectiveness

A report by the Universities Funding Council Information Systems Committee Courseware Development Working Party stated in 1992 that,

the scale of investment required is such that until a clear and enduring strategy has been agreed, most HEIs will be reluctant to embark upon the massive infrastructure investment and major structural changes that are required to make the transition that programmes like Teaching and Learning Technology are trying to bring about (ISC, 1992).

This same report also found that 70 per cent of academics would be interested in using computer-based teaching programs and that they identified advantages such as:

- dynamic visual presentation;
- provision for rehearsal of basic skills;
- improvement of learning and understanding;
- access to data and information sources;
- saving of staff tutorial time.

There is no doubt that the costs will be high if we are to achieve the educational and time gains which are possible. A quick glance through the Phase 2 TLTP projects indicates the amount of money needed for developments in very limited parts of courses. First year costs of £250,000 for core history resources, £80,000 for a few video optical discs of images for teacher training, £135,000 for computer-aided teaching about concrete and £230,00 for the development of human-tutor emulation software for teaching introductory financial and management accounting, are typical (TLTP, 1993). Most of these costs are based on existing hardware, and many are only adapting existing software packages rather than producing a completely new package. This means that real costs of developing IT-based courseware will be much higher than these figures might suggest.

It is difficult to find a measure of cost-effectiveness from present projects because they are a combination of research and development. While this is the case, and academics can write up the work as research papers, the enthusiasm is high. The rest of the academic community within HE will be asked to spend this time later on, probably without the funding now available, developing computer-based materials. The overall balance between research and teaching would come under great pressure if the time investment were not properly financed and recognized.

Experience from developing flexible learning materials suggests that producing one 'student hour' of material takes 10 hours for audio, 50–100 hours for written and 300+ hours for video materials (Crabb, 1990). For IT-based flexible learning we would need to add to this the capital investment in providing enough workstations and replacement hardware, network infrastructure costs, and the costs of updating courseware to match updated hardware about every four years. It does not take long to reach large costs for small parts of courses to develop the image-based courseware which the new technologies are increasingly capable of handling, and which would be required to maintain educational parity with conventional teaching methods. Better authoring systems will reduce development costs, but even so the high costs and required time commitment would suggest that educationally sound flexible learning environments on a large scale are a long way off. There is the continual danger that,

developments driven by technological possibility can sometimes take place without much attention being paid to explicit theories or models of learning. For example, hypermedia learning materials may often be produced in a climate of untested optimism. It is sometimes assumed that this type of information presentation is likely to be in some way effective – without any empirical test of the assumption (Ford and Ford, 1992).

I will let Adman and Warren (1994) have the final say on costs to higher education:

Finally, a cautionary remark: no amount of money poured into a new venture can guarantee its success. In reaching out for quality learning via educational technology, institutions have the responsibility to ensure that any new investment made in this area produces real efficiency gains without diminishing funds for crucial research activities and existing support services. That, clearly, would be a folly.

Conclusions

When considering all the issues, there is little doubt that as hardware and software develop, and the IT infrastructure extends, more flexible teaching and learning styles will also develop. There are fundamental learning enhancement reasons for this – the power of such systems to facilitate the flow of information and the evidence from research, at all levels of education, that our IT can enhance learning.

There is also little doubt that we should be experimenting with what is available as it develops in order to be in a position to capitalize fully, in terms of maintaining and even improving teaching and learning, on technological developments as they arrive. As an on-going research activity, such experimentation and development are welcome and rewards can follow. At the moment the time commitment needed for individuals and institutions to develop IT for teaching will inhibit its extensive use. Advocates of wholesale use of IT primarily to reduce the unit costs need to take a more holistic view of the full effects of major changes to teaching and learning processes in higher education.

References

Adman, P and Warren, L (1994) 'A strategy for educational technology in higher education', *Journal of Computer Assisted Learning*, 10, 1, 50–54.

Crabb, G (ed.) (1990) *Costing Open and Flexible Learning: A practical guide*, Coventry: National Council for Educational Technology.

Darby, J (ed.) (1992) 'Authoring systems for courseware development', *CTISS File 13*, University of Oxford.

Davies, P, Scarborough, S and Brailsford, T (1992) 'Authorware Professional: multi-platform icon authoring', *CTISS File 13*, pp. 7–11, University of Oxford.

Davis, N and Wright, B (1993) 'Learning spin skills', *Times Higher Education Supplement*, 19 November.

DES (1989) *Information Technology and Initial Teacher Training (The Trotter Report)* London: HMSO.

DfE (1992) *Information Technology in Secondary Schools: A review*, London: HMSO.

Ford, N and Ford, R (1992) 'Learning strategies in an "ideal" computer-based learning environment', *British Journal of Educational Technology*, 23, 3, 195–211.

Gardner, J and Munroe, G (1992) 'Authoring and authoring systems', *CTISS File 13*, pp. 45–6, University of Oxford.

Garrett, B (1992) 'Flexible learning in the 1990s', *CTISS File 11*, pp. 26–7, University of Oxford.

HEQC (1994) 'Checklist for Quality Assurance Systems: A briefing from the Higher Education Quality Council', London: HEQC.

ISC (1992) *Beyond Lectures: The report of the Information Systems Committee Courseware Development Working Party*, University of Oxford: CTISS Publications.

NCET (1993) *The Future Curriculum with IT*, Coventry: National Council for Educational Technology.

Saunders, M (1986) *Trends, Influences and Future Curriculum Provision*, Guildford: Future Curriculum Trends Working Party, Southern Examining Group.

Sealey, M (1994) 'Not like a book', *Educational Computing and Technology*, 15, 2, 9–12.

Searl, M (1993) 'Campus without walls', *Times Higher Education Supplement*, 19 November.

Sivajnanam, C (1993) 'Libraries without walls', *Educational Computing and Technology*, 14, 8, 18–19.

TLTP (1993) *A Report on 33 Additional Projects*, Bristol: Higher Education Funding Council for England.

TVEI (1991) *Flexible Learning: A framework for education and training in the skills decade*, Sheffield: Employment Department.

Chapter Four

Off-site Support for Flexible Learners: Learning in No Man's Land

Alison Smith and Winnie Wade

Maintaining the flexible learner

This chapter discusses some of the infrastructural issues involved in mounting a flexible approach to teaching and learning with a focus on mature students who are released on a part-time basis by their employers. The point is made that support is a key issue in developing a quality experience. Many of the problems encountered by such students are, however, relevant across the range of flexible learners. The case is made for directing greater resources towards the non-classroom elements of a course where there is a danger of flexible learners becoming invisible learners or non-learners.

The support context

Flexible learners will be, to some degree, autonomous or semi-autonomous learners. They are outside the comfort zone of tutor control which is a feature of traditional learning. Autonomy suggests that students will be self-sufficient; it is, however, the contention of the authors that, in order to be successful, the autonomy of flexible learners requires support. For the purpose of this discussion, flexible learners are not those who learn solely through the traditional classroom-based route, neither are they learners at a distance. Flexible learners are those who employ a variety of learning methods specific to their individual needs and, as such, their requirements are unlikely to be met by a standard approach to teaching or to support.

Success criteria for flexible learning must be more than simple output measures of graduating students. Arguably, qualitative success measures must be employed if students are to be attracted to flexible approaches; the quality of the learning experience is important and flexible learning must not be viewed as a poor relation of classroom-based teaching either from the provider's point of view or the student's.

Who are the flexible learners?

Off-site learners are emerging in all academic areas. They span the extremes of full-time school and undergraduate students to part-time, mature, professional and postgraduate learners. They may be on- or off-site for the whole or part of their course of study. If off-site, they may be engaged in distance learning, project or research work. Alternatively, they may be undertaking a work placement, 'on the job' training or working quasi-professionally as a student teacher, or medical house officer.

Mature students as flexible learners

Thorley (1991) points out that the numbers of students aged over 21 entering higher education institutions are rising and, at the time of writing, were a quarter of the total numbers. These students enter a system which is oriented towards younger learners and they are likely to find themselves in a minority within the course group, unless they are entering a course specifically designed for mature students. Amongst groups of 18–20-year olds who enter higher education more or less straight away from school, the more mature, non-standard learner may well be isolated and experience a lack of confidence.

Returning to an alien form of learning

In traditional learning settings, mature students often experience difficulties in returning to learning; the discipline and skills required to study effectively may have been forgotten. Additionally, those whose early education took more of a vocational than an academic path may feel disadvantaged. Traditional learning tends to have an obvious structure and system which may give the hesitant mature student confidence and security. In flexible approaches, responsibility for learning may appear to rest more squarely with the student and support is an issue which must be tackled if mature flexible learners are to enjoy a positive and successful experience.

The 'non-standard' stigma

Mature learners, so often valued for their experience and insight, can also be encumbered by other commitments and are therefore potentially less focused in their study. There is, of course, the maxim which puts forward the alternative view: 'If you want something done, ask a busy person.' Wisker (1991) acknowledges statistical evidence which demonstrates that mature students, in this case Access students following pre-degree preparatory courses, achieve good degrees but also indicates that providers remain nervous of a group which they still feel threatens standards and the status quo.

Study skills

Successful flexible learning needs to be underpinned by a sound study skills base. These study skills must be learned within the overall context of the learning. The essence of flexible learning is that individuals learn in different ways using a range of approaches and displaying a range of attitudes. Two main approaches to learning have been identified (Gibbs, 1992):

● The surface approach – the student reduces what is learnt to the status of unconnected facts to be memorized. The learning task is to reproduce the subject matter at a later date.
● The deep approach – the student attempts to make sense of what is learnt, which consists of ideas and concepts. This involves thinking, seeking integration between components and between tasks and 'playing' with ideas.

The deep approach can be developed in flexible learners by helping students to acquire and recognize their own study strategies (Entwistle *et al.*, 1992).

Flexible learning, by its very nature, needs a wide range of support, some of which can be achieved through study skills. Study skills required by flexible learners will be both general and subject-specific. Students should be given help and advice in thinking about the way that they study. They should be offered 'alternatives from which they can select methods which they find congenial and helpful' (Entwistle *et al.*, 1992). Central provision of study skills support can be offered, but study skills are most relevant within the context of the course and integrated into it. Giving the flexible learner the opportunity for individual tutorial help on study skills, if required, is also important, as is peer support through self-help groups.

The need for a service culture

Accommodating different needs and approaches to learning is a must. Wisker (1991) identifies the importance of starting from the standpoint of the learner rather than delivering simply what the provider has to offer. Flexible learners may well have very specific reasons for taking a course of study; they are unlikely to have a great deal of study time at their disposal and may well be demanding students, expecting high delivery standards and specific content.

They are likely to be intolerant of tutor-oriented and controlled lecture sessions which may provide only a performance platform for academics to expound personal hobby-horses. They want and need to be engaged in learning as a cooperative activity and the lecturing role may need to be redefined as facilitation. Naturally this has implications for staff who are unwilling or unable to adapt.

Student-centred learning and assessment

Increased numbers of flexible learners will inevitably force changes in both teaching and assessment. Collection of evidence for portfolios and records of achievement have recently become established as forms of assessment (Tallantyre *et al.*, 1992) and learning contracts and personal development plans are being introduced in both private and public sector organizations. In terms of teaching approach, the group dynamics of any course group vary from cohort to cohort and the presence of even one flexible learner will have an effect upon the way the group is taught and learns.

The development of student-centred approaches seems obvious yet Farrington (1991) claims that there is considerable talk and many claims to student-centred approaches but very little substance. Whatever happens on a course is driven by an agenda set by tutors with learning packages designed by them. The tutor remains in control and there is little negotiation. Students are not autonomous, only using the tutor as a resource, although it can be said that the best teaching is where students say, 'We did it ourselves'.

Clearly, true student-centred learning demands a degree of maturity and responsibility on the part of the student, the ability to know what it is necessary to learn, and to negotiate means of acquiring the required knowledge and skills. Farrington (1991) has concerns about the soundness of giving a great deal of emphasis to the learner and his or her intentions and, while arguing that students must be at the heart of any educational activity, is also unsure about giving too much freedom and choice. A balanced flexible approach must value the qualities, skills, knowledge and attitudes which the students bring to the course of study and use these as starting points for development. Supporting the student to make informed, useful choices and decisions must be a crucial element in the process.

The above are common themes in flexible learning from which more specific issues evolve in relation to particular groups of mature flexible learning students. A summary of our own learning about the support process from a group of flexible students on a postgraduate course at Loughborough University follows.

Learning from flexible learners

The postgraduate diploma in business management comprises a mix of classroom teaching and off-site learning. The flexible approaches centre primarily upon self-managed learning through guided reading, and assessment through work-based projects. The students are in full-time employment and are scattered at company locations across the country. Their attendance at the University is part-time. Growing awareness of the off-campus challenges faced by this group led to research which focused upon their learning at work, at home or in any location other than the university – their learning in 'no man's land'. The main features from this project, which have applicability to a wide range of flexible learning situations, are summarized below.

Management of the process

Dealing with company students is different from dealing with mainstream, full-time students. Significantly, they are referred to as 'participants' rather than 'students'. This small detail immediately places them in a different category of learner and this has implications for programme management. Full-time students within traditional learning can be regarded almost as patients in a patient/doctor relationship with lecturing staff. Lecturers drive and control teaching in traditional situations and, as Farrington (1991) claims, even in student-centred learning, students are rarely autonomous. Company student/participants however expect that their experience will be valued by the lecturer and expect to participate in their own training on a more equal footing. Management of this relationship is therefore an issue and lecturers need to be aware of the subtle differences involved and their implications for successful learning.

Students sponsored by employers demand and receive a high degree of service and care both during the taught elements of the course and off campus. Their level of satisfaction with the course itself is naturally related to the quality of customer care. Giving and maintaining high levels of customer service has resource implications for the provider and is particularly challenging when students are not physically on hand and easy to contact.

The participants also demand a taught learning environment which is more training than education and the theory-practice debate is a live issue here. Paton and Lay (1986) identified a difference between the learning aims of academia and industry, ie, that industry's emphasis is fundamentally upon application and outputs rather than learning itself. Smith (1993), reporting on a study of employer attitudes towards the MBA qualification, also highlighted the sponsors' demands for the development of practical competence to be treated as a priority. The academics involved in the delivery of a sponsored programme have to juggle the demands of maintaining academic standards and the demands of the participants for industrial credibility and practical applicability. Lecturers need to be less 'ivory tower' and more 'hands on' in their attitudes. They need to have had industrial experience and maintain links with industry in order to be credible.

Practical application is as important in the design of the distance learning and assessments as it is in the classroom teaching. Lecturers whose distance learning materials are perceived as philosophical, conceptual, obscure or 'academic' come in for strong criticism, particularly if other lecturers within the same subject area have been able to adopt a more practical focus. While uniformity of approach is difficult to achieve, and is perhaps also not desirable, clearly tutors who teach mature professionals and become involved in flexible approaches need to be aware of the different demands which will be made of them and be responsive to those demands.

The management of the flexible learning process is not, in the case of company courses, solely a matter for the provider. The company, as sponsor, needs to take an active part. This stage of management development cannot simply be handed over to the provider and then taken back once the course is over. While the support given by the company training manager is paramount, it is unlikely to be sufficient and the company will gain more benefit if it involves other key people. Mentoring is one important way of gaining support and involvement more widely.

Mentoring

Off-site learners often need advice, encouragement and support as part of the process of learning. This can be provided by a mentor, a wise counsellor in a neutral position who could be a trusted colleague or fellow student having regular contact with the learner away from the place of learning. Mentoring is frequently used as part of the learning process in industry and commerce and is now a recognized practice in higher education.

Flexible learners working at a distance can find such a person a great support especially with respect to such aspects as:

- providing support for the learning process;
- giving feedback;
- preventing the learner feeling isolated;
- being positive and encouraging;
- helping maintain motivation;
- assisting in the planning of work.

The establishment of a mentoring system needs to be approached carefully. In any effective system there should be trust between student and mentor. The mentor should be able to help the employer recognize the worth of the student engaging in the learning process and in the linking of the academic world with the work environment. She/he should also help the learner cope with external pressures that are not directly related to work or study, such as family problems.

The student employees comment that mentors are particularly important in reducing the isolation which many experience during the programme. They are sometimes critical of the mentor system which the company sets up, stating that the mentors were often too busy to fulfil their role adequately. There is a general view that while senior management support for the programme is evident, middle management support is less strong. More senior mentors were requested in order to achieve easier access to the information participants required to carry out their assessed work successfully and to act as a buffer for them. These students clearly saw the mentoring role as one of advocacy.

A number of students feel that a more integrated approach to mentoring, ie, one which involves the university both in the initial establishment of the system and liaison between mentors and tutors, would make the programme much more beneficial to employees. Specifically, closer links would improve the taught material by making it more company-specific and greater knowledge of and input to the projects would improve dissemination within the company. The transfer of learning for the students themselves would be increased and there would be contribution to profitability by implementation. Project mentors from the employers are seen as vital to the successful application of the project within the organization.

It is important that mentoring does not happen in a vacuum and for the tutor to assist the mentor and student to agree a structure to the mentoring process. It needs to be consciously managed. Options to be considered include timetabled mentoring, informal mentoring through frequent casual meetings, peer mentoring and telephone mentoring (Race, 1994).

Mentor training is important and both employers and providers are becoming increasingly aware that mentoring skills are not something managers are born with. In many organizations training is provided for mentors to prepare and support them for the task ahead. Recently-graduated student 'survivors' may well be excellent mentors, and graduates of the programme in the study volunteered to act as mentors for the subsequent group. This group may be more in tune with the current students and understand the processes and problems better than the experienced practising manager.

Having identified two key protagonists in the support triangle – 'education provider' and 'work sponsor' – it is important to examine the third protagonist in the relationship and the part played by peers (both fellow students and, in the case of employee students, colleagues).

Peer support

Peer support can provide an invaluable aid for off-site learners. Part-time students often feel isolated and do not receive as much feedback as they would like. Self-help groups can be set up either formally or informally to meet together to provide an essential mutual support for the learning process. Ideally, group size should be no more than six and groups should be structured so that individuals are able to meet out of working and college hours. Gibbs (1992) describes how self-help groups or 'study networks' were set up in a part-time course. Students saw the networks as increasing motivation. Three stages of network formation and support were described:

● stage 1 – team building;
● stage 2 – taking part in business simulation games which helped promote cohesiveness;
● stage 3 – focus on analysis of group processes and the development of effective working practices.

Establishing peer support groups can be difficult when the students are scattered. Students are usually dispersed and work in quite different circumstances from each other; some are office-based and sedentary, others, engineers for instance, often work at remote sites for months at a time. This latter group usually feel they suffer most, both from lack of networking opportunities and inability to carry out any study while at work because there are simply no facilities available to them. (There are doleful comments made that only the office-based participants gain distinctions.) Variable learning conditions inevitably impact upon the learning. Designing assessment which acknowledges these variables is an additional challenge.

It is useful to suggest that the employer needs to formalize student peer support groups by the establishment of learning sets which are given time to meet. An extra day at the university should be set aside without any timetabled teaching. This would allow groups to meet and function, give reflection time (which is scarce in the taught elements) and allow participants access to the library. Inevitably such a suggestion involves considerable extra cost both in terms of accommodation and opportunity cost. However, some means of facilitating a learning network needs to be given careful consideration. Networking serves both to reduce isolation and to reduce workload by sharing books and company information and contacts.

There are pitfalls in peer support which can be minimized if sufficient time and resources are employed at the beginning to set up peer groups carefully. Team building activities should identify problems or potential problem areas such as the individuals who dominate, or the 'lone rangers', and appropriate action should be taken. A good group structure takes time to set up and if not managed, groups may fall apart. Once in place, peer groups need to be monitored and eased through any difficulties. They cannot be left entirely to self-management particularly where the group may be lacking in confidence and may eventually feel resentment that tutor support has been taken away.

The attitude of work colleagues is another issue. While it cannot be expected that they should get involved in the learning to any great degree, they need to be prepared for a situation where their colleague is not always physically there or may be at work but engaged in study activities. If the work environment is not adequately prepared there may be resentment. On the other hand, supportive colleagues can be invaluable in enhancing the learning for the individual student and in sharing the experience in a receptive work arena.

Institutional support

In a situation where students are part-time and sponsored by their employer good institutional support is a necessity. The support given by the company has already been touched upon in the section on mentoring and peer support. However, the issue is a wider one which ideally involves a partnership between sponsor and provider.

The company

In the case of the company, it is necessary to provide a more supportive working environment. Time should be given during the working day for participants to undertake coursework and use distance learning materials. The provision of physical space for study in the working environment is important. Workloads could be made more flexible so that the balance of academic and company work can be more easily achieved, avoiding conflict between course assessments and particularly busy work periods. Work rotation where all participants have at least six months placement at head office, and thus easier access to senior people and information, would be helpful. Availability of internal learning resources encourages learning.

It is necessary to ensure that staff within the company recognize the value and benefit derived through part-time study. This will prevent peer jealousy. Looking towards the future, students often feel unsure as to the company's plans for them. What does participating in the course and achieving the award mean in company terms? Can students afford to fail? What are the likely benefits to the individual of passing? Past students of the course can be used to give a more positive company context to encourage participation.

The provider

The providing institution also has a responsibility. Tutors need a better understanding of the industry in order both to make their material more relevant and to appreciate the working environment and its demands upon participants. Company visits can be made prior to each module to assist tutors in their appreciation of the nature of the students' work and texts should be geared specifically to the industry.

Tutor accessibility is a key issue, as is the provision of a dedicated administrator to respond quickly to queries. A pattern of tutor contact should be established from the beginning. Student advisers could be appointed who would contact participants regularly and clinic sessions could be timetabled. If tutors record their lectures on to tape the flexible learners feel more confident and secure.

Materials support provided by the tutors can provoke considerable comment concerning the amount of reading required and the lack of uniformity in the guidance given. The required reading is regarded as heavy especially since, in many areas, participants are starting from a very low knowledge base and are expected to achieve a high level of understanding. Detailed feedback on the materials is essential for both making improvements in the future and for enabling the provider to understand better the students' needs.

A consistent comment from students concerns the nature of the materials support vis-à-vis their position as part-time, flexible learners. It is often their view that the provider needs to give much more guidance than would be the case with traditional learners. 'Spoonfeeding' is the phrase regularly used. This need for spoonfeeding conflicts somewhat with the broadening and challenging philosophy of university education where the individual might be expected to develop their own judgement in learning. This situation also calls into question the notion of self-managed learning. For some students the course can be a type of company-sponsored training and thus a means to a largely company-determined end; the request to have all the information given is thus understandable. In designing support materials a balance needs to be achieved between satisfying what appear to be student survival demands and the academic requirements to stretch the student mind.

Institutional support, in this specific case, also extends to the library. Access to the library is difficult for those who live at a distance and use of a short-loan section is impossible. The library often is not able to send books to the students and many find that even if they manage to take out books at the end of a taught module, these books will rapidly be recalled. They are able to use other libraries close to home for reference but there is often no agreement with other higher education libraries which would enable them to borrow. Students in remote areas may not have even the reference facility. While all required reading should be supplied, students consequently find it difficult to read around the subject and to gain additional information useful for their projects. For these participants, the difficulties with library support are a priority issue.

Conflicting demands

The differing pressures exerted upon students in this kind of situation should not be underestimated. It is very easy to think of students only as they appear in the lecture room. While it can be argued that the students know what they are undertaking, many find, at times, the pressure of juggling home, work and study very great. Participants are often nominated by their company because it is felt that they have considerable potential. Managers so labelled tend to be given more responsibility, not less, and allowance should be made for study. As well as work, these students may have partners and a family who may not understand and appreciate the difference it will make to their lives. Family support and commitment are thus important to off-site learners.

It is evident that a number of the support issues raised at the beginning of this chapter are relevant to the off-site learners but, of specific importance, is the interrelationship of the major stakeholders. In establishing a company training programme it is easy to develop a strong liaison related to course design and delivery – the tangible 'up front' elements. It is clearly crucial to pay as much attention to the softer interpersonal elements which provide an all-round support network to the whole process. Getting this right improves the quality of the experience for the learner and is thus more likely to lead to student success.

There are undoubtedly general lessons which can be applied to the spectrum of flexible students. Principally, these are related to tailoring of support material – making the medium appropriate to the group, understanding the situation of the flexible learner and how it can assist or hinder the learning process, identifying and responding to flexible learners' needs and assisting the development of appropriate support mechanisms. These issues are not peripheral but central to the cause of making flexible learning an attractive and first-choice option.

References

Entwistle, N, Thompson, S and Tait, H (1992) *Guidelines for Promoting Effective Learning in Higher Education*, Edinburgh: Centre for Research on Learning and Instruction.

Farrington, I (1991) 'Student centred learning: Rhetoric and reality', *Journal of Further and Higher Education*, 15, 3, 16–21.

Gibbs, G (ed.) (1992) *Improving the Quality of Student Learning*, Bristol: Technical & Education Services.

Paton, R and Lay, C (1986) 'Learning to manage and managing to learn', *Open Learning*, 1, 3, 18–21.

Race, P (1994) *The Open Learning Handbook*, London: Kogan Page.

Smith, A J (1993) 'The controversial MBA', *Training Tomorrow*, October, 23–5.

Tallantyre, F *et al.* (1992) *Portfolios as Assessment Tools within Higher Education*, Red Guide Series 2, No. 1, University of Northumbria at Newcastle.

Thorley, L (1991) *Support for Mature Students in Higher Education*, SCED paper 64, 57–62.

Wisker, G (1991) *Facilitating Access to Higher Education; A student centred approach*, SCED paper 64, 49–55.

Chapter Five

Course Guides for Flexible Learning

Keith Hodgkinson

Introduction

Recent changes in the structure and teaching of programmes in higher education have made the development of more comprehensive and flexible course guides an urgent necessity. Reliance on a single 'course book', often a dense, didactic and deadly textbook, plus over-long reading lists, is no longer sufficient to provide quality guidance through learning routes. Courses have become more complex with increasing modularization and course options. Epistemological changes create new learning needs: tutors demand computing and discussion skills, research tasks and presentations, report writing and managerial exercises, fieldwork and off-site placements. Individual routes through course options are more difficult to negotiate successfully, and non-traditional students may be at particular risk in such circumstances.

This chapter on the design of flexible course guides is based upon a constructivist model of learning. By this is meant the view that the most effective learning occurs when students actively build new ideas (concepts, information, skills and attitudes) into and onto their current knowledge. Good learners can then construct new ideas in this process – they transform the nature of their own understandings or schemata. Ideas become more subtle, more complex and more advanced – but learners remain active agents, making their own contributions to the process rather than just passively memorizing someone else's words or symbols. This model of learning emphasizes the importance of taking account of individual learners' motivational and other psychological needs. Course guides therefore need to be:

more	*and less*
attractive	serious
supportive	instructive
user-friendly	dense
interactive	didactic
varied	uniform

They should:

- support the teaching content;
- give a clear sense of direction and progression;
- offer frequent rewards and comfort;
- encourage student thinking, reflection and involvement.

The best teachers aim to make their students independent learners. Kember (1991) said, 'I like to think of a study guide as a tutor sitting alongside a student reading the textbook'.

Costs and benefits

A full course guide takes much longer to prepare than a series of lectures. Rowntree (1990) suggests 50 hours for a complete (ie, one-year) self-contained course. This is probably an underestimate, particularly for a beginner. Few lecturers can be provided with such large blocks of free time. Wright (see Chapter 12), more realistically, spent some six to seven months producing his first distance package for an MSc course. The task was complicated by the need for collaboration between technical author, text editor and graphic designer. The latter's importance, function and priorities should not be underestimated, particularly for coherent package format and design. Training in information technology skills was unexpectedly time-consuming: 'One hour of student material took approximately 30 hours to prepare and, because computer software is frequently upgraded, needs almost constant revision'. On the other hand, the geography project (Chapter 7) found the production of a revised and extended course guide for just one short undergraduate module to be much less burdensome.

The combined experience of recent flexible learning projects is that a guide to a shorter, modularized course may take less time, and complete multimedia packages will take very much longer. Guides for the more flexible and therefore more complex courses will need longer and more expensive preparation. Collaborative writing has the potential to create more variety and there will be some time savings provided all contributors keep to an agreed agenda and house style. Designing a guide for a new course is easier in some respects than re-vamping an old and well-established one. There are usually fewer compromises to make and fewer people to please. Content can be tailored to individual needs and to local conditions.

Specific benefits to students offered by suitable guides should become obvious as the course develops. They may include improved levels of commitment, motivation and final satisfaction and should therefore lead to higher or at least equivalent levels of learning. Tutors should be freed for longer periods from the pressure to respond to the needs of individual students, although increased motivation may lead to higher levels of student and student–staff interaction on a task. Unfortunately it may be extremely difficult to demonstrate experimentally that flexible course guides do improve learning since few tutors would be willing to teach parallel groups with and without an appropriate course guide. Comparisons with the work of previous student groups is never reliable as the variables are not controlled. Cost-benefit analysis should therefore be focused on qualitative improvements in terms of student course ratings and staff satisfaction.

Full costs, including staff time for negotiating, writing and redesigning, are rarely worked out in detail. There is a dearth of literature on cost-benefit analysis in flexible learning in further and higher education, of which work on producing course guides forms only a part.

Types of course guide

There are several different kinds of course and study guide:

- a guide to a specific activity or project;
- a guide to a text or a set of textbooks;
- a technical manual;
- a collection of readings or extracts;
- a guide to a course of lectures plus reading and seminars;
- a guide to lectures plus readings/extracts, seminars, activities, course-work;
- a guide to off-site activity (work placement);
- a complete course guide, with or without associated course text.

A guide to published materials is probably easier to write than a structured reworking of one's own. For the former, authors can choose the best material, various points of view or alternative explanations, and show different kinds of diagrams and illustrations. Or they can juxtapose contrasting opinions or explanations and let the students use those they find most suit them. Such a guide may be little more than an enhanced annotated bibliography. But it can include questions, tasks, comparisons and summaries. The style can be brief, chatty and challenging in order to offset the academic style of most published texts.

Using other people's textbooks can cause problems. There are questions about the suitability of text, access to sufficient texts of the same edition, hard or paperback, and the management of updates. Wright, for example, makes clear his apprehensions about some aspects of the chosen text, and his course guide provided critical corrections (see Chapter 12).

Using extracts (papers, chapters, articles) is easier in this respect. Updates and modifications are more easily managed and stylistic differences give an added attraction. Students find such collections more fun – they can browse, skim and select according to their own interests. Designers should aim to choose extracts – or chop up big extracts – so that students can read one, complete, in 20-30 minutes (the average concentration time of a motivated adult learner; note the length of Open University TV programmes, or of programmes between adverts). A really good collection in a new area can be published. All collections should be checked for copyright.

The design process

To reorganize an established course or to design a new one from scratch can be a complex exercise and needs careful planning. The process of doing so in order to meet flexible needs is best achieved collaboratively, preferably after discussion with experienced students. Foster (1993) provides a comprehensive framework for the management of course design while in this present volume, Brown (p. 81) gives insight into the practicalities.

The following action plan sets out the main stages in the process.

1. Set learner objectives. Note that these are not the same as teaching objectives: what the tutor teaches is not the same as what the student learns. Learning can be analysed as information, concepts, values, skills or experiences. Such objectives should be set out clearly at the start of the guide and should be used for reinforcement and motivation during progress through the course.

2. Identify core content and define its structure. On the assumption that the syllabus and the main content for the course are already available, the key question will be to identify the central concepts or experiences and to create a flexible structure for student learning. Which elements may be optional or elective, which are peripheral, which will need reinforcement or further development?

Flexible elements need to be clearly identified and additional support offered when choices need to be made.

3. Decide on assessment procedures and timings. Choose from exam (progress or terminal), coursework and projects. Allow time for private or syndicated study, for revision and for feedback. Is assessment to be formal and summative, or diagnostic and formative?

4. Write the first draft. This will take up most of the time and energy. Reading other or similar course guides will help. Experience suggests that for every hour spent writing text, authors will need to spend about three hours in editing and redrafting.

5. Find and select support materials. A written introduction will be required, placing materials in context and explaining their significance to the learner and to the learning objectives. (A later section deals with the question of contents.)

6. Layout and design. Outlining the layout and graphics for the technical draft and source materials is a major design task. Technical support should be available to deal with highlighting of key ideas, blocking and boxing and the use of consistent colour and icon coding.

7. Pilot draft. A first draft, with graphic input, will then have to be piloted with a sample and is probably best done with students who have just completed the course. Modifications will need to be organized, including possible graphic and technical changes.

8. Print and package. As with the graphic and design stages this will have to be organized well in advance with plenty of allowance for unforeseen delays. Again, it will be the course tutor's responsibility to check for copyright, noting the need to label materials according to current regulations.

9. Evaluation of course guide. Annual review procedures should be built in to the process by inviting or even requiring student annotations of the guide itself.

Providing a structure

In non-fiction books the contents page lists the sections in the order in which they should be read. The content sequence is linear or hierarchical, running from the simple to the complex, from the known to the unknown. Later units build upon and are therefore dependent on the learning that has been achieved in earlier units. Such a structure builds confidence and encourages students to persevere, but it has two disadvantages:

● it assumes that all students have indeed fully understood and are ready to move on, together, to the same point and at the same rate or point in time. It is clear that students do not all fit into this model of learning sequencing. Illness, for the simplest example, could seriously disrupt student progress;
● it makes no allowance for brighter students who may wish to proceed more quickly, or for those who have prior learning of some units, or those whose interest may be aroused by the subject or nature of later units. In all three cases a linear progression would apply a significant brake to their learning rates.

Most academic teaching follows a linear structure for discrete, single-subject elements or modules. Even the most straightforward course structure needs to have to respond to communication difficulties and illness: the reality of resource management in higher education often breaks up theoretical linearity. More flexible courses that do not follow an obvious sequence and content should be mapped more openly, allowing for personal choice from a broad menu. Off-site conditions are even more unpredictable and so distance guides should be even more carefully prepared. Course design within the Open University, for example, has undergone a revolution since the first study unit 'tombstones' appeared.

What flexible students and their tutors most need is a critical path analysis or a concept map of the course. Key issues here are the design of simple block diagrams to show structures, and the consistent use of deadline markers, locational cues, signposts for cross-unit links and feedback and escape routes. Accreditation systems, off-site placements and career outcomes (particularly where course options are offered) also need to be included.

Student support – the importance of the introduction

Students who are asked to carry out a lot of work on their own will need a lot of psychological support. They need three kinds of reassurance: that the course manager/author is ok (reliable and legitimate), that the course is ok, and that they are ok.

Welcoming notes should introduce the course tutors (their background, experience, qualifications and interests) and the course itself. Students need to know how new it is, or how well-established, what previous students thought, who validates it, how many will pass, how interesting and useful it is. What will they gain from it? What can they do with it?

The course rationale must be explicit. Objectives should be itemized, possibly with a more friendly approach: 'At the end of the course you will be able to...We do this because... You will have to do that in order to... This comes first because... Last year the students said they wanted...so this year we will...'. A diagram of the course design offers much reassurance, particularly when work deadlines are clearly marked in.

To reassure students about themselves, they may be reminded about the competition for entry. They could then be asked to fill in a personal profile at the start in order to identify strengths and weaknesses and plan their time management. Another anxiety is raised about their chances of passing a course. They need to be told how to do so and thus it will be very important that the criteria for assessing each requirement are set out so they know precisely what they will get their marks for.

A list of chapter headings and an index give little idea of the significance of each unit, the provenance of text and of key ideas. The introduction could include a lively commentary: 'Unit 1 was written by ... who first began this work in the USA....The readings here come from professional journals and newspapers and show how varied are informed opinions on the matter...This section is very short but contains one really important idea...'.

Finally, an introduction should also explain the escape routes (telephone numbers, student contact groups) for when things go wrong and early priorities need to be highlighted.

For students on industrial placement there will be concerns about accommodation, links to the university and access times for tutor and pastoral support, and the management of the placement. A separate booklet or section should be provided for the placement mentor who should in any case be given the same course guide as the student. A 'placement guide' could include material and advice from former students, for instance, 'How mentors can best help their students'. Off-site support is discussed elsewhere in this book (Smith and Wade, Chapter 4).

Course guide contents

Most of the course guide content will probably consist of academic text or a running commentary on other authors' texts (extracts, chapters, etc.). Such content is necessary but not sufficient for a flexible learning context. Additional material should be provided for three reasons. First, long blocks of information can be difficult to digest, so breaking up the sequence of academic text is always a useful tactic. Second, students will appreciate, and some will only appreciate, information in non-text form, via visuals (diagram, map, picture, graph, etc.) or through other forms of writing (notes, reports, comments). Finally, students will need a more personalized guide to text indicating the author's and eventually the student's individual relationship to the content.

The importance of graphic input cannot be overemphasized. Race (1992, sections 23 and 24) provides a list of ten good ideas, with notes:

1. Give your learners a break.
2. Give them something to hang on to (especially with new ideas).
3. Help them to make sense of what they have learned.
4. Show them what cannot be described in words.
5. Show inter-relatedness (between and within units).
6. Collect ideas together.
7. Show them where they are.
8. As a task [Race gives several good ideas here].
9. Encourage them to develop their own diagrams and images.
10. Humour!

For study of visual or kinetic subjects, graphics can be essential. One potential danger, though, is access for visually impaired students: alternatives can be provided as indicated in Chapter 1.

The following non-standard material could thus be added to conventional academic text:

- maps, diagrams, pictures, graphs, charts, cartoons, etc.;
- book reviews and summaries, by students and other professionals;
- samples of student work;
- working sketches, tutors' handwritten notes, diaries, interview transcripts or other dialogue, extracts from reports, etc.;
- summaries and conclusions;
- questions, problems and puzzles.

Writing and writing style

Research on the reading problems of students has enabled educational authors to write more effectively for a much wider audience. For teaching purposes, and especially where flexible and non-standard students are concerned, the central concept to be borne in mind is that of text readability. Readability has little to do with the content of text in terms of its complexity, detail or length, and everything to do with print, word length and grammatical structure. A number of software packages now offer text readability analysis but these are not always reliable, particularly where technical terminology is used extensively and, moreover, repeated, since repetitions can lower readability levels. It is also important to note that the readability level of text, given in terms of age, should be below the average student age or ability level.

Font size and type can be crucial and both can easily be varied. Word and sentence length are the other major factors in text readability. Authors should try to provide shorter substitutes for any word longer than three syllables – and it is surprising how often this can be achieved without significantly affecting meaning. Many long technical terms are essential to the content, but their repetition has progressively less effect.

The combined effects of word and sentence length are discussed in the literature on readability. Of several tests and techniques available, the simplest and easiest to apply without using computer software is the 'Fog index' as described by Colin Harrison in Gilliland (1977).

Grammatical structure also has a dramatic effect but is a factor that is often ignored in computerized readability assessment. Subordinate clauses and even phrases, such as this one, should be avoided wherever possible because, apart from increasing sentence length, they also tend to induce confusion through their complexity and so will require long attention spans which stretch even the most avid adult readers, however skilled and highly motivated, as those who have attempted to read Proust will recognize. Point made. So keep sentences simple. It is best, also, to keep to the present and/or past tenses. Subjunctives (should, would, might, could, etc.) and complexities (ought to have been...) create difficulties especially for over-seas students. Next, avoid indirect speech ('Indirect speech should be avoided'); 'In the Victorian period factories were built...' is not as readable as 'The Victorians built factories...'. Using direct speech also reduces sentence length. Finally, authors may occasionally address their students directly. This can make an immediate impression – yes?

Interaction: student tasks and assessment

Much research into the effectiveness of teaching and learning techniques has shown the importance of the idea of student interaction with text and other materials. Essentially, students should be invited to make contributions to the text itself, either by reacting to it in discussion, research or other off-text activity, or by actually adding to the text in writing. Current terminology is the SAQ or Self-assessment Question.

Setting SAQs within the course guide reinforces learning, adds to the overall variety of the guide and increases student involvement and motivation. Tasks may be intrinsic to the reading such that students can only proceed intelligently by having completed a task. Or they may be extrinsic to the text, incidental and additional to the reading and involve students in off-guide work and extension activity. Finally, they may be formal in that they make a contribution to the final course assessment, or informal and thus, to some extent, optional. The purpose and relevance of all tasks should be clearly stated and, if formally assessed, the marking criteria should also be declared.

The following list of tasks is derived from various courses and literature and does not distinguish between formal and informal assessment. Tutors may use them for either:

1. *On-guide tasks:*
        add to text
        underline
        fill in box
        sentence or diagram completion/extension
        cross out
        correct errors (but query for safety and technical exercises)
        add a variable.
    Comment/evaluate (often by pair/small group discussion):
        pick out strengths/weaknesses
        preferences between alternatives
        interpret
        criticize
        summarize/report on.
    Problem solving:
        find correct solution
        make decisions
        make predictions
        assess solutions offered
        choose from alternative solutions
        accept, modify or reject ideas
        offer explanations
        work out example.

2. *Off-guide – individual or collaborative:*
        collect data
        ask questions/conduct survey
        draw diagrams/plans
        fulfil design brief
        test solutions offered
        compare results with text
        assess theoretical statements in the field
        construct theories from field data
        read and summarize text(s)
        review literature
        find examples.

3. *Making reports and presentations.*

Tasks can be self-paced and set within workshop or even lecturing time. Assessment of student tasks can be made by the students themselves, by peers or other colleagues and professionals/mentors, by tutors of course, or not at all. Self-assessment is becoming increasingly popular for diagnostic purposes but requires careful planning. One (information technology) project found that,

Model answers with indications of likely mistakes needed to be written. Students needed encouragement to be constructively critical of their own and their peers' work, and to seek assistance if they did not understand (Hall and Saunders, 1993).

Within mass higher education systems it is becoming common practice to assess by lecture/course attendance, lecture summary submission, or by ticking boxes, with computerized scoring. Flexible assessment via a choice of task options is a further advance towards genuinely open learning.

Finally, student interaction may be used to good effect by inviting individuals or groups to annotate current course guides. Knowing that their responses are to be built into next year's course can boost student commitment. This can produce very positive and even creative suggestions, and student awareness of wider issues of course rationale and structure will also help course development and appreciation by the student body. The course guide to flexible learning should itself be flexible.

Conclusion

Existing course guides for traditional courses in higher education already contain many of the ideas offered in this chapter. Not all of them will be relevant for all types of course and course guide. It is important therefore to be able to identify those elements which are characteristic of and will encourage flexibility.

Course guides can provide for flexibility in a number of ways. Most of these are to do with access, routes, facilities, assessment and structures. But the central processes of teaching and learning sometimes remain inflexible. A culture of tutor dependency is created and sustained partly, it must be said, by student collusion and encouragement.

Clearly the induction process will be very important in complex courses and for non-standard students. Orientation does not stop at the end of week 1, however. At each stage, wherever student options and choices have to be made or new commitments undertaken, where they are required to work alone or in the field, they will need further reassurance through confirmation of progress and reaffirmation of direction and strategy. Constant and positive feedback is required, and the skills of and confidence in critical self- and peer assessment will need to be taught and encouraged.

Central to flexible learning is the process of creating or selecting individual pathways to learning, with or without tutor assistance and counselling. Students usually find that the best resource is often their peers, and the sharing of experience, mistakes and achievements needs to be built into the course structure and rewarded. Space must be provided for continuous student reflection and occasional celebration. Learning habits, techniques and styles will vary enormously and course guides must acknowledge students' rights to their own learning agenda.

References

Foster, G (1993) 'Managing course design', *British Journal of Educational Technology*, 24, 3, 198–206.

Gilliland, J (ed.) (1977) *Reading: Research and classroom practice*, London: Ward Lock.

Hall, J and Saunders, S (1993) 'Some lessons from a student-centred approach to teaching and learning', *British Journal of Educational Technology*, 24, 3, 207–9.

Kember, D (1991) *Writing Study Guides*, Bristol: Technical and Educational Services.

Race, P (1992) *53 Interesting Ways to Write Open Learning Materials*, Bristol: Technical and Educational Services.

Rowntree, D (1990) *Teaching through Self-instruction; How to develop open-learning materials* (revised edn), London: Kogan Page.

Chapter Six

Flexible Learning and the Library

John Arfield

Introduction

Flexible learning has received increased attention in universities as it has become seen as an important element in any strategy for coping with the sharp increases in the number of students entering higher education. These increases place strains on teaching accommodation, as universities struggle with insufficient seats in lecture halls and other teaching rooms. They place strains on academic staff, who, while needing to improve research performance and output, must cope with larger groups of students and increased amounts of marking and assessment. They place strains, too, on libraries, which face more students in need of books, study spaces and assistance.

From this point of view flexible learning may be seen merely as a device to shore up the ability of the higher education system to produce a greater number of graduates. Yet flexible learning should rather be viewed as a means of improving the effectiveness of education. Seen from this more positive perspective it complements the library's central role in the education of a student. An educated society is a society whose members have developed the capacity to think independently and critically and who are able to find and to use information. In this the ability of an individual to use libraries effectively is essential; the more that a student's education fosters this ability the more valuable his or her education will be.

As a central resource supporting teaching and learning, the library is intimately concerned with changes in the process of education. Changes in the population using the library, changes in the methods used in teaching and learning, and changes in the technologies that can be used in the learning process all require the library itself to change and to adapt the services it offers to ensure that they are appropriate and meet the needs of its users.

Changes will affect the library service in a number of ways. The characteristics of the users of the library will be more varied than in the past, the type of material required will be different, the development of information handling skills will be more important, and the involvement of library staff in the delivery of education will be critical.

Changing users, changing needs

Students

It is likely that the users of libraries will be more varied than in the past. Courses which free students from the necessity to attend university full-time and which enable much more flexible patterns of study may attract people with backgrounds that are very different from the school-leavers for which courses have in the past been designed. They may have a wider range of experience and a different level of motivation (McElroy, 1988). Universities are developing courses which attempt to open access to study for students from commerce and industry whose primary entrance qualifications are experience and potential rather than academic qualifications. Such students may be returning to learning after a considerable period of time, they may not previously have followed an academic course of study, they usually have full-time jobs and are likely to have family responsibilities. Some courses are intended to meet the needs of both full- and part-time mature students. Typically these students have had no recent formal education, have a high level of motivation but also a higher level of doubt as to their ability to cope with the learning environment.

For such people traditional library opening hours, loan periods and reservation arrangements may not be suitable. In order to protect the interests of students who are unable to attend the library during the day it may be necessary to set up separate collections. It may be necessary to have special sessions in the evenings to give instruction in the use of information, and to have senior library staff available at such times to deal with reference enquiries. As students come to rely increasingly on access to information which is available to them via computers rather than through the printed page, the technical support that they will need must be available to them when it is required. Students with other commitments and demands on their time will be less able than full-time students to visit the library themselves. Documents may need to be delivered to them either by post or electronically. Library staff may need to provide more of their service over the telephone and special arrangements may be required to enable such students to reserve or renew books. Access may need to be provided over computer networks to data or programs which are in the library. Those who do not arrive in 'learning mode' may require considerable amounts of support and advice from library staff at times when such assistance has not traditionally been available.

Teachers

Teachers themselves may find that they have new needs when they are faced with developing flexible learning strategies. The library may need to provide relevant books and journals on the subject of writing courseware, using new teaching methods and constructing learning packs. Examples of material that has been developed elsewhere will also be a useful source of ideas. There will need to be close liaison with any initiatives the university may set up to promote flexible learning strategies. It may be appropriate to establish a separate collection of such material, to publicize it and to find ways to promote its use.

Changing methods of teaching and learning

Flexible learning is a term which covers a number of techniques and approaches to teaching, all of which may have different impacts on the library, and to which the library may contribute in different ways. The key features which these techniques have in common are that a variety of teaching methods beyond lectures and seminars are used and that individual students are required to play a greater part in the direction and pace of their own learning.

Distance learning techniques

The central problem of distance learning – the delivery of courses to students who are at a distance from the university itself – is how to provide the materials that students need. There may be a need for a postal service or the setting up of small regional libraries. It may be necessary to seek to establish reciprocal arrangements with other university or public libraries. Course material in the form of pre-printed notes or specially prepared course textbooks may be produced. Where these involve reproducing extracts from published work there may be issues of copyright that will need to be resolved. The current copyright agreement in the UK between the Committee of Vice-Chancellors and Principals and the Copyright Licensing Agency, acting on behalf of most rights holders, stipulates that study packs which contain *four or more* extracts of copyright material in sets of *five or more* must be cleared for copying through the CLA's telephone service CLARCS. Payment will be required. This agreement is in force until 31 July 1995.

Some of the techniques of distance learning may be applied within an institution as lecturers are less able to spend time with their own students. At the beginning of a course pre-produced course workbooks may be distributed to students, who are then able to work through them at their own speed. Insofar as these workbooks avoid the need for students to use the library to find their reading, they reduce the pressure on libraries. Such workbooks might, however, contain reading lists or set assignments that require increased use of the library.

Libraries themselves are being forced to consider using such techniques in order to give guidance to students on their use of the library. It has become extremely difficult to give introductory lectures or tours to large groups of new students; there have been a number of responses to solve this problem. Some solutions have used introductory videos or tape-slide guides. Some libraries have developed introductory packs for distribution to new students. At Loughborough University tours conducted by library staff are now confined to groups of students, such as part-time or foreign students, who can benefit from the specialized assistance that can only be given by library staff (Davies, 1993). All other new students are encouraged to take a copy of the library's self-guided tour. This printed leaflet leads a student through the library by way of points which are clearly and prominently signposted; at each point the guide gives a clear and concise explanation of the key features. This method has the advantage of greatly reducing the amount of library staff time that is devoted to introductory tours; but it also has the considerable benefit from the student's point of view that the tour can be taken at the time and speed that is convenient and appropriate to the student, and allows parts to be repeated at will. In the first year of use the guide was publicized only to new students, but it soon became clear from comments received that second- and third-year students also wished to use it.

Project work

Another key feature of much flexible learning is to encourage learning by finding out or by doing. This can be a much more effective way of learning than merely being told facts. It often takes the form of project work. This approach places the onus on students to find information for themselves. This gives rise to the need to find relevant information in a usable form within defined time constraints. The skills developed in achieving this are important in themselves quite apart from the direct benefit to the project work. Project work may also require students to gain knowledge and skills that have not been taught as part of their foundation work. This approach means that much greater demands are made of the professional skills of library staff as the need to impart information-handling skills becomes increasingly important and as they deal with more frequent, more specialized and more varied requests for assistance in finding information.

Projects may not only be undertaken at the individual level; they may also be given to groups of students. This can give a taste of collaborative research, and can also draw on the capacity of post-experience students to learn from each other. Such students may prefer to work at home or in the library. The library may therefore need to provide study space where group work and discussions can take place without causing disturbance to other library users.

Information technology

Information technology has added new dimensions to flexible learning. The use of computers allows learning materials to be delivered directly over networks and enables a two-way flow of information. Modularization can result in very large classes for common units. This can cause intense short-term demand for set texts. A recent report from the higher education funding councils has suggested that delivery of such texts electronically may be part of a solution to this problem (Joint Funding Councils' Libraries Review Group, 1993). Interactive video and computer software permit learning without the direct intervention of a teacher, and expert systems can be used to enhance learning. Students' work can be submitted electronically and be returned with marks and comments by the teacher. Teleconferencing and e-mail can remove some of the constraints of physical distance from the teacher. The delivery of information and learning resources, whether they are physically held in the local library, or remote, opens up new possibilities for teachers. The essential pre-condition for successful use of these possibilities, however, is ready access to computing facilities for all who need them. The cost of providing and maintaining these facilities is one of the major problems in realizing the potential of new technology.

Changing libraries

Reading lists

It is likely that conventional reading lists will continue to play an important part in flexible learning courses. There is often a wide gap between the perception that tutors have of the function of books in the learning process (and therefore their expectations of students) and the perceptions of their students, who are often unwilling to read any more than what is absolutely essential or to look any further than what is available in the short loan collection. Lecturers may provide reading lists which are unrealistically long and undifferentiated. It is crucial that library staff should have reading lists well before they are used by students in order to ensure that sufficient copies are present in the library's stock (although it is not easy to estimate what the likely usage of titles on reading lists is likely to be). Reading lists also provide evidence to library staff of how a course is likely to be organized and what the impact on the library is likely to be (Graham, 1986). However, the library is rarely able to rely entirely on reading lists for an indication of the impact of a course: lecturers frequently make verbal additions to the printed list, often fail to give any indication of the relative importance of the titles and fail to notify the library of any special assignments which they may give students.

For reading lists to become more effective, however, there will need to be an active participation by the library in feeding back to lecturers information about the use of their reading lists. The library is in a good position to do this. There is a tendency for students to concentrate on the real syllabus (ie, the minimum that needs to be done to get a satisfactory degree) rather than the published syllabus, and to confine their reading accordingly. Student requirements of course guides include a wide choice of readings, an indication of the location of library materials, clearly defined *essential* readings for each week and the identification of the most relevant page numbers when a whole book was given as a reference. Although this tendency is regrettable it is a fact that cannot be ignored. In the light of information provided by the library, teachers might reduce the amount of reading expected of students, earmarking, for example, sections of books rather than the whole work and expecting less of the student's own discrimination. Information from the library on how reading lists are actually used should result in more effective lists.

As undergraduates gain increasing access to computing facilities, reading lists may be consulted on-line. When they are integrated with networked library catalogues it is possible to see whether a book is on loan, when it will be available, and to reserve it. The ability of computers to record the use made of reading lists will enable monitoring and provide information on how they are actually used. Students will be able to comment on reading lists, requesting the supervisor for further or alternative reading or asking questions.

Book stock

The demand that will be placed on the library's book stock will vary according to the subject being taught and the teaching methods to be used. In some subjects at some levels an appropriate strategy for a teaching department might be to eschew background reading altogether in favour of teaching from a single textbook. Students will be expected to purchase their own textbooks, or may be lent a copy by the department, with little effect on the library. In other subjects there may be intensive demand for books, requiring extensive use of a short loan collection.

Increased use of project work may mean the library having to provide a wider range of reading than might have been required for a course relying heavily on textbooks and introduces an element of unpredictability into what books may be needed. If projects are within a narrow range and are repeated each year, the library may be able to support them adequately as long as sufficient advance notice is given. If there is a wide range, or if students are able to choose their own projects without prior investigation of the support that they will require from the library, they may find severe difficulties in obtaining the material when it is needed.

In the near future readings themselves may be accessible online, avoiding congestion for the printed version. There are crucial questions of copyright to be resolved; once they are, and students have ready access to terminals, the effect on library services could be dramatic.

Non-print media

In addition to books and periodicals the library may find itself with an important role in providing other forms of information. The library may be asked to house course packs and student essays. Although hitherto the use of audio-visual material in teaching has not been as widespread as was once predicted, videos, audio cassettes and multimedia packages may all need to be accessible in the library. This in turn may require greater invest-ment in space and funding for playback equipment. It may also require a re-examination of the relationship between the library and the university media services department. In some universities library and media services have been amalgamated into a single service unit.

Computer-based services

The library will be required to house a wide range of books, periodicals, audio-visual resources and computer software. In addition the library will wish to enable students to gain easy access to resources outside the univer-sity. Students working on projects may need increased access to the inter-library loan service. Computer teaching programs and packages developed at one university will be generally available to the university community. Libraries and computer centres will need to work together to ensure that students have access to them. The broad bandwidth provided by SuperJANET will enable video and audio to be delivered across the network. Data banks and other resources available over the Internet may be relevant to students working on projects; library staff will need to give advice and guidance on what is available and how it may be used.

Information-handling skills

Clearly courses which rely less on the direct provision of instruction by teachers in classrooms and more on students taking responsibility for conducting their own learning make it essential that students should know *how* to do this. Study skills need to be provided early in any course which requires students to take more responsibility for their own learning. Academic staff themselves have the primary responsibility for this, and they must ensure that students are equipped and prepared for the active part they will be expected to take in their own learning. None the less library staff have a unique role to play in providing students with appropri-ate skills in seeking and handling information. Experience has shown that in order to be effective, training in information skills should be integrated as an essential part of a course; should have some results in that the train-ing should be directly related to the broader aims of the course; and should actively involve students. It should also have some reward, with successful completion of this part of the course contributing to the ultimate success of the student. How this can be accommodated by staff who are already busy and who will be increasingly in demand to answer the specific enquiries that will arise from increased amounts of project work and increased use of networked information sources is a critical question for librarians.

Librarians and the educational process

Monitoring and assessment

Above all the successful development of flexible learning within a university requires that the library and its staff should be closely involved in the process at all stages. It cannot be assumed by course designers that the library will have the resources to meet the new requirements that such courses may bring. At the same time there may be possibilities for the creative use of library resources which may be overlooked in the absence of a member of the library staff. At the very least there must be ample information given to the library at an early stage so that it can assess the library support that will be required. But much better is a realization that library staff are partners with academic staff in the teaching and learning of students and that they have a distinctive and important contribution to make. With this sort of integration into the university's teaching process the library's own experience of how students use libraries in this process can be fed back into the design and revision of courses. For this to happen both libraries and academic departments need to have a clear view of the intended outcomes of a teaching programme. The current emphasis on assessment of teaching quality aims to introduce a cycle of improvement. That there should be so little attention paid in assessment procedures to the role of the library as a key element in a student's learning experience is a serious omission. Libraries must organize their resources and their staff in such a way as to build strong links with teaching staff and their courses so that they are used to greatest effect.

References

Davies, E J (1993) 'The hitch-hiker's guide to the academic library; the development of a self-guided tour at Loughborough University of Technology', *Library Management*, 14, 7, 4–13.

Graham, T (1986) 'University libraries, students and reading provision' in Baker, D (ed.) *Student Reading Needs and Higher Education*, London: Library Association.

Joint Funding Councils' Libraries Review Group (1993) *Report*, Bristol: HEFCE.

McElroy, A R (1988) 'Resourcing and supporting open and distance learning: some educational and managerial models', *Learning Resources Journal*, 4, 3, 100–112.

Part Two: Flexible Learning in Action – Individual Case Studies

Introduction

The case studies presented in this section are concerned with the range of approaches to the development of flexible learning across a selection of university departments. These case studies explore a number of issues concerned with flexible learning. They discuss the need to develop more innovative approaches to teaching and learning as it has impacted upon the teachers and students within various departments. Practical ways of addressing these needs have been piloted and evaluated and many of the departments are now going on to a second stage of development where the pilot study moves from being experimental to being part of the teaching portfolio and new ideas are being developed to pilot stage. The cases demonstrate a growing confidence that flexible learning approaches can be beneficial to students and exciting for teachers.

In many departments, it is fair to say that flexible learning began as a potential solution to a problem, an initiative to help staff cope with the recent dramatic increase in numbers. As such, it was imbued with all the negative connotations which are associated with changes in conditions. While it is too early to say that a sea change has occurred, a philosophy is emerging whereby considerable numbers of staff now regard the initiative as positive and exciting and are actively looking for new ways to enhance the learning of their students. These case studies reveal the range of attitudes towards flexible learning in its early days within one institution and are very open accounts of the situations and issues with which staff have grappled. As live examples, we hope they will be interesting and of use to staff in other institutions who are seeking new ways of meeting student needs.

The issues which the cases raise are broad and varied. Specifically, each case deals with an individually funded project to look at a particular aspect of flexible learning pertaining to a subject area. The contributions from the English department and the business school involve a wide-ranging discussion of the issues which need to be considered when applying innovative teaching methods. These areas include identifying the client, a needs analysis, consideration of the circumstances in which students work and the diversity of the student group. Similarly, the geography department project, in addressing new ways to approach the teaching of large groups, identifies a number of associated considerations. Flexible teaching will also require the development of new approaches to assessment, and new ways of resourcing courses. All of the projects highlight the fact that flexible approaches require students to accept greater responsibility for their learning and that this is a concept which needs to be well embedded if such an approach is to be successful. Both the business school and the education department projects highlight the responsibilities of others in the learning process: namely students' industrial sponsors if they are funded by a company and teachers in schools who are now having to play a greater part in the training of successive teacher generations. Cases from design and technology, maths, education and engineering design give concrete examples of the piloting and implementation of discrete flexible learning packages for particular groups of students. Their experiences provide valuable lessons for those whose ideas are still at the conceptual stage and who wish to learn both about the learning package itself and the methodology of trialling the project with live students.

These examples, all from one institution, demonstrate the variety of need and the requirement to be creative in higher education. This particular institution is still learning from its Flexible Learning Initiative and will no doubt continue to do so in its quest for innovative, high-quality approaches to the development of students' learning.

Chapter Seven

Coping with Larger Classes: Flexible Learning in Geography

Ed Brown and Jonathan Beaverstock

Introduction

This chapter outlines the response of a geography department to the challenges of expanding student numbers over recent years. It details the development of a project, initiated in October 1992, designed to explore ways of coping with larger class sizes without compromising a long-held commitment to innovative and imaginative forms of teaching.

Context

Along with most other geography departments in Britain, the geography department at Loughborough University of Technology has recently been faced with a marked expansion in its undergraduate population. While the first-year intake is only now approaching the one hundred level, the expansion that has occurred has been quite dramatic, representing a three-fold increase in four years with only two additional members of staff.

This shift in staff–student ratios has led the department to expend considerable time and energy in a far-reaching review of its teaching programme. Within this process two factors have been prioritized: first, the maintenance and expansion of individual student choice and, second, the continued provision of a wide variety of learning experiences for students. These concerns have led to a continued emphasis upon small-group teaching, despite the greater demands on staff time it embodies.

A review was initiated during the 1991/2 session when the department took the opportunity offered by the introduction of the university's modular teaching scheme to extensively overhaul the range and structure of the courses offered to undergraduates. This led to the implementation of a modular degree programme in the following session which involved the introduction of a series of new module types. Most of these modules reflected the continuation of traditional lecture-seminar based taught courses, practical classes and field courses. This study, however, concerns a new flexible module type, much less intensive in its use of staff time, introduced at that time. This module type was designed to be efficiently resourced in order to guarantee the continuation of other more traditional modules with a high element of staff or student interaction. The new modules now constitute half of each student's total modules in their second and third years of study. They are timetabled for one two-hour block a week (foreclosing the possibility of running separate seminars), are formally assessed through end-of-year examinations only and, through the mechanisms of student module choice, also encompass the largest class sizes.

In October 1992, through a grant under the university's Flexible Learning Initiative, a project was launched within the department to explore the development of these new modules, to assess the types of teaching strategies appropriate to them, and to review the particular problems and opportunities that they represent.

Major issues

The project was devised to address a number of fears concerning the development of the new modules. Such fears related to a perceived lack of opportunities for feedback and discussion given the large numbers of students involved on the modules, the lack of personal contact time between staff and students, and the absence of formal coursework. As these new modules represent 50 per cent of each second- and third-year student's studies, the concerns described led several members of staff to express serious reservations about their educational value.

Aims and objectives of the project

General aim

To maintain the overall quality of students' learning experiences during the development of the new modules in the department, through the identification of effective teaching strategies and the encouragement of active student learning.

Specific objectives

- To widen the range of teaching techniques on the new modules via the examination of different strategies of coping with larger class sizes and the encouragement of active student learning;
- to identify by interaction with staff (and students) strategies which would be both accepted and effective;
- to develop an increased range of informal assessment techniques.

Anticipated outcomes

- An increase in the quality of teaching and the effectiveness of the department in coping with an increasingly large number of students;

- the development of an extended range of assessment techniques;
- better use of staff time;
- adoption of teaching and assessment techniques developed through the project throughout the department.

Process and outcomes

Throughout the first two years, the project has encompassed a number of different activities.

Review of published material

An exhaustive review of materials relating to flexible approaches to teaching in geography was carried out. A wide range of materials has been consulted and catalogued and will eventually be published as an annotated bibliography. In addition, a resource collection has been developed which is available for staff to consult within the department. The rapidly growing literature dealing with the problems associated with this topic was summarized, for example, in recent editions of *The Journal of Geography in Higher Education*, CVCP (1992), PCFC (1992) and Gold *et al.* (1991).

Staff seminars

Ideas have also evolved through a series of staff seminars. An initial meeting produced a lively general discussion where both the advantages and the pitfalls of the new modules were discussed in depth. Building upon this, further meetings have discussed detailed responses from staff about their own experiences as they have administered and taught the new modules, examples of their support materials, and their ideas for future developments (especially in terms of novel forms of assessment and the encouragement of group interaction).

One of the most important issues that emerged from these discussions was that although the new modules were designed to limit staff contact and marking time, they should be able to play a complementary role to other more intensive forms of staff–student interaction through their placement within a properly thought through module structure. The modules do have their own educational advantages in that they can be used to encourage students to take greater responsibility for monitoring their own progress and organizing their own time and, moreover, they also require innovative approaches from lecturers which may serve to expand, rather than restrict, the range of teaching activities.

Student survey

A detailed survey of student opinions about the new modules was carried out toward the end of the 1992/3 academic year. Opinions were sought in general regarding the human geography module and physical geography modules and regarding one specific example of each ('Geography of the global space economy' and 'The Holocene'). Approximately 65 second-year students completed the survey. The intention of the survey was not simply to respond to student preferences but rather to give the students an opportunity to outline their anxieties and concerns about the new modules. The implications of the findings from the survey have been used to inform appropriate strategies for the continued development of the modules. Some of the more important observations are detailed below.

Teaching techniques

One of the survey questions related to student views on the teaching methods employed by lecturers during each two-hour block of the module. There was particular interest in feedback from the students on the various alternatives to using the timetabled period as a two-hour lecture. In general, the responses suggested that imagination and variety are the keys to student satisfaction. There appeared to be strong feelings against lecturing throughout the two-hour period emanating from some, though not all, students and it was felt (acknowledging the problems of room design and size experienced by some staff) that there is a need to identify and develop a broad range of teaching strategies. A number of alternatives were suggested to the students in the survey: a further hour's lecture, small-group discussions, discussion amongst the whole class, practical exercises, quizzes and tests, videos and films and role play simulations. The views collected from the students have been used to inform staff discussions on the continued development of teaching strategies on the modules.

Assessment

Further survey questions related to students' concerns over the absence of a formal coursework component to the modules. Responses showed that while students had a certain anxiety regarding a lack of feedback on their progress, by no means all students expressed this strongly. When asked about what forms of assessment they would like to see on the modules, students were generally in favour of some form of formal, as opposed to informal, assessment (especially essays, presentations or projects). Obviously the reason why these do not exist on these modules is the intention to limit staff time spent on marking so that detailed coursework requirements could be maintained within the other module types. None the less, innovative forms of informal and formal assessment could be found which do not involve large amounts of staff time.

There was strong support from the students questioned for some form of self-assessment exercises to be used on these modules. These could be attempted in many different ways; for example sets of questions on each lecture could be included within a much extended course guide (or given out weekly to guide reading), or periodic multiple-choice tests or quizzes could be carried out. Such activities could be beneficial for most modules.

The development of specific modules

Three members of staff have met regularly to review the development of
the new modules and to pilot innovative ideas for the way in which these
modules will be run in future years. The student surveys have been evaluated in detail and three quite different approaches are being developed.

In the first, one lecturer has focused upon the production and utilization
of a detailed course guide (including extracts of reproduced articles, exercises, reading lists, detailed course requirements and lecture outlines) in
conjunction with student feedback on its future development. The time
spent on producing such guides is not excessive and, given the lack of
personal contact between each student and the lecturer, may be one of the
more efficient ways of improving the quality of these modules. The recognition of the importance of detailed information and the provision of
clearly articulated requirements is also serving as a base from which to
develop effective course guides for other modules. The new course guides
are also used in field studies. Detailed guides have been developed on a
second-year human geography field course in Northumberland and a
physical geography field course which takes place in Switzerland. The use
of these guides has been tremendously effective in nurturing active student
learning in groups on these modules.

In a second module different ways of encouraging group interaction in
the second of the two timetabled periods is being explored, along with
ideas about informal assessment techniques. This has been pursued
through the use of six student-led groups. Each of these groups has taken
responsibility for one of the 'second hour' sessions, during which they have
made presentations and led discussions on material that is not covered
directly in the lecture programme but is, none the less, examined. This
provides the incentive for students to complete the tasks given, despite the
lack of formal assessment.

This strategy has been developed in coordination with the piloting of an
interactive computer-based resource, the STILE project (Students' and
Teachers' Integrated Learning Environment) as an alternative to a detailed
course guide or reading list. This system provides students with access to
information for the modules they are taking, as well as relevant illustrative
images. In future years it is intended that the system will allow for
computer-based interaction between students, and between the lecturer
and groups of students, without the need for actual timetabled classes.

A third module, Industrial Restructuring in the British Space Economy,
has also developed more effective means of informal assessment, evaluation and innovative teaching methods employed in each two-hour session.
The aim of this module was to provide the students with various explanations regarding the geography of industrial change in Britain during the
last 20 years. The module incorporated three major elements: the theoretical perspectives associated with the nature of industrial geography; the
emergence of the service economy and new forms of regional policy, labour

markets and entrepreneurship; and a focus on high-tech industries. The structure and organization of the module is outlined below.

The lectures presented in the module outlined the main trends and generalizations of industrial change in the British Space Economy, 1970–93. However, for the final year examination the students were required to have detailed knowledge of regional case studies as well as the national trends. This information was not given in the lectures. Instead, the second period of every week was set aside for *group work* on a regional case study. In this way, the students could unpack the distinctive geography of change in each of the United Kingdom's standard regions. The students were required to work together in groups of five and disseminate their findings to the rest of the class in the form of a poster presentation and report. Although the poster and report were *not assessed* they contained information needed to answer a compulsory question in the examination.

Group work was emphasized as being a very important element of this module. The students were given the responsibility for supplying the rest of their group, and the class, with information. It was stressed that the only way in which they could learn effectively was through their working together. This was achieved through the students bringing material about their region to the class for discussion with the rest of their group. The tutor was available in the class to discuss any aspect of the group work and provided a regular slot in the timetable for personal tutorials.

The poster presentation outlined the *key trends* of the geography of economic change in a United Kingdom standard region between 1981 and 1993. In contrast, the report, a five-page document, outlined in detail the geography of economic change in that region. The format of the report included:

- a detailed examination of the region's changing industrial base and labour market;
- a map outlining the geography of change;
- a reading list for the rest of the class.

The group reports were photocopied for each member of the class.

Reference material for the class was listed in the detailed handout. Other key sources listed included: HMSO data (for example, *Regional Trends, Social Trends, Economic Trends*) ; regional journals (for example, *Regional Studies, Geoforum, East Midland Geographer*); and the *Financial Times, Economist* and other financial periodicals.

Discussion

The initial period of this project has seen the exploration of a number of different facets of the development of these new modules. Staff have discussed in detail the problems that they have experienced and the successes they have had; the opinions of students have been sought in some detail; wide-ranging resources have been collected and a number of different approaches to the running of the new modules have been attempted. The review of our experiences has revealed considerable success in how the department has adapted to the new form of teaching. Obviously the acid test of the success or failure of the modules will come from an extended review of examination performances and more detailed feedback from colleagues and students, both of which are being carried out at present.

One point that emerged from the survey responses was that students are generally antagonistic toward the use of non-traditional methods of assessment or informal methods which do not count towards their degree. In particular, self- and peer assessment (even when formalized) are not popular and, more surprisingly, neither is the assessment of group work. Bearing this in mind, and the need for students to take more responsibility for their own learning on these modules, it is imperative that students are introduced to new methods of working at the outset of their university career. To this end a first-year study skills module is being developed which, in conjunction with the established tutorial system, will introduce students to the different types of assessment used in the department, the dynamics of working in groups and the need to take responsibility for their own academic development.

Conclusions

The project described in this chapter is part of an ongoing process of adaptation in the department and new ideas continue to be developed. The centrality of open discussion and the sharing of experiences amongst staff is seen as crucial and the series of staff seminars is being continued and expanded to include the sharing of ideas from visiting speakers from other geography departments and elsewhere. Further detailed evaluations of the department's first experience of these modules are also being carried out through a formal survey of staff, further questioning of students, detailed evaluation of exam performances and the comments of external examiners.

While still in an exploratory phase, two issues of wider relevance can be highlighted from the experiences which have been outlined in this chapter. First, decreasing staff–student ratios, despite having peaked in the last academic session, are likely to be a continuing feature of university life. Our experiences suggest that it is important that the reaction to such changes involves a thorough review of teaching methods if a commitment to student-centred learning is to be maintained. Second, while lecture-only modules were at first viewed in the department simply as a cost-cutting exercise for coping with increasing student numbers, the experiences reviewed here suggest that it is more useful to view them as a means of increasing the variety and quality of teaching approaches and encouraging students to take a greater responsibility for their own learning.

References

Committee of Vice-Chancellors and Principals Universities' Staff Development Unit (1992) *Effective Learning and Teaching in Higher Education*, A series of twelve modules, Sheffield: CVCP.

Gold, J R, Jenkins, A, Lee, R, Monk, J, Riley, J, Shepherd, I and Unwin, D (1991) *Teaching Geography in Higher Education: A Manual of Good Practice*, Institute of British Geographers, Special Publication Series, Oxford: Blackwell.

Polytechnics and Colleges Funding Council (1992) *The Teaching More Students Project*, Oxford: PCFC/Oxonian Rewley Press.

Chapter Eight

A Flexible Learning Strategy for Design and Technology Students

Joyce Cubitt, Tony Hodgson and Eddie Norman

Introduction

Traditional approaches to the teaching and learning of design and technology are becoming more difficult to sustain and the need to consider alternative strategies is becoming more urgent. A number of factors have contributed to the need to consider strategies intended to be more flexible and accommodating:

- worsening staff–student ratios;
- the need to provide an increasingly wide range of technological information at the relevant point of design development;
- a belief that design students and teachers are entitled to relevant technological knowledge in a form which is appropriate to their needs.

This case study describes the selection, development and evaluation of trial materials which aim to support individual student learning in design and technology. The initial student groups were identified as first-year industrial design and technology undergraduates undertaking foundation studies. This target is continually widening, however, and might eventually also include students aged 16–19 taking advanced level design and technology in schools and colleges and teachers who wish to develop their own technological capability through in-service studies.

Context

Design and technological activity tends to employ a very wide knowledge base and consequently students are always making use of subject areas beyond their immediate expertise. This knowledge base is conventionally divided between the sciences and the arts. Scientifically based designers might need to draw on areas associated with product semantics, aesthetic awareness and human factors, and arts based designers might need to consider aspects like materials selection, energy use, manufacturing and electromechanical system design. Our initial project has been concerned with the scientific knowledge base of design, but this should not be interpreted as indicative of our long-term intentions. The overall aim is to explore the potential of flexible learning for all aspects of design and technology. The use of departmental resources, including lecturers, would be a key element of the materials and so they would not be suitable for use in a distance learning mode.

The aims of the project as originally stated relate to these issues and can be summarized as:

- primarily to support individual student learning;
- to support the maintenance of high quality learning experiences with declining human resources;
- to facilitate the acquisition of individual knowledge and skills at the point of need.

During the project there has been a gradual shift of emphasis which is concerned with a growing interest in the idea of *entitlement*. Design students or teachers *should* be able to access information concerning relevant technological ideas if they need to. Traditional textbooks often contain the required information, but they are in a highly condensed format and normally require explanation. Centres of expertise, like colleges or universities, can provide courses, but these require attendance. Designers need to understand technological issues in order to select appropriate technology, and have to be able to gain access to the necessary skills and knowledge, but the traditional approaches to the teaching and learning of technology do not serve designers well.

Gibbs (1992) showed that 'if active use of information is not made shortly after the lecture then much of what was originally retained is lost'. Teaching in design and technology has always pursued active learning approaches, but Gibbs also showed that even when the knowledge was applied only 50 per cent is likely to be retained in the longer term. Design courses have sometimes sought to teach aspects of the appropriate knowledge base through foundation courses, but it seems unlikely that year 3 students will remember much of the work covered in year 1 unless it has been in regular use.

Energy was the first topic we would consider for a number of reasons:

- it is a vital area for designers both in terms of awareness of issues and the capability to perform technical calculations and assessments;
- it is an area where the prior student learning is very diverse, arising from subjects like physics, geography and design and technology;
- it is a 'free-standing' short course in the summer term of Year 1 Industrial Design and Technology at Loughborough University.

The first two reasons imply that, if successful, there will be major benefits to both the students and the department. The third was particularly important in that if the trials were unsuccessful the resulting damage could be easily limited. Hopefully the teaching and learning in the autumn and spring terms would be unaffected, and revision 'lectures' could always have been organized before the exams.

Process and outcomes

Developing a flexible learning resource is a major undertaking and it was immediately decided to seek external support. It was not considered to be practical for already hard-pressed teaching staff to write the necessary materials. Sponsorship was obtained from British Gas. Teaching staff provided all their notes and ideas, which the author undertaking the contract was free to make use of. However, the author appointed was also an experienced lecturer, and therefore was able to suggest and research additional material. Numerous discussions were held to establish the required nature and content of the materials over a period of several weeks before writing began. Review meetings were held regularly during the writing period, which lasted approximately three months, and feedback given continuously as the materials were developed. Regrettably there was not enough time for any piloting before the trials began. The author was employed as a lecturer during the trial period, which provided invaluable continuity and support.

We were also fortunate in that a flexible learning initiative had been launched across all departments independently and simultaneously. This provided access to two flexible learning consultants who were employed by the university. Clearly, advice was sought from them, but also from the Supported Self Study Unit in Northumberland which has five years experience in producing materials targeted at GCE A and AS level students. The questions to which we were initially seeking answers fell into three areas and examples are given below:

1. What is the distinction between flexible learning and distance learning?
    Did some areas of the unit need human intervention and feedback whereas others could make use of structured feedback built into the materials?
    How do we identify and classify areas of the material that cannot be put into distance learning textual material?
2. How can we ensure that the learning materials fulfil our aims?
    How can we create suitable diagnostic procedures to ensure that the material is truly flexible for students with differing backgrounds?
    Would different learning materials be required for students with different backgrounds, eg, mature students?
3. How can we ensure that the study units are used effectively?
    Should there be an initial teacher input and, if so, how long should it be?
    Should there be tutorials at set points in the course to cover extra material or to pick up on student problems, or should they be by request only?

After consultation and consideration of these questions we were able to arrive at a number of policy decisions. We decided to:

- write a *flexible*, rather than a *distance*, learning package;
- provide only the support material for a current text (Norman *et al.*, 1990);
- use a diagnostic exercise to assess previous learning and plan the most appropriate learning route;
- provide a short initial teacher input to help students work through the self-study materials;
- provide a main folder of learning materials to be retained by the department and separate sheets for students to keep;
- provide as wide a variety of activities as possible, in addition to self-assessment questions;
- encourage group discussion and activities;
- provide glossary sheets to help students collate important information;
- use different media where appropriate;
- teach all students as flexible learners and not have a 'control' group for the purpose of research evaluation;
- use this initial project to determine the most appropriate staff intervention in flexible learning materials.

Many of these decisions could be the subject of extensive discussion and the following notes only touch on some of the more important issues. Effective flexible learning depends on good guidance and clear agreement on appropriate objectives between the teachers and the learners. Hence the need for planning sheets to record objectives and well-documented activities and resources. Clearly guidance is available from lecturers at tutorials, but instructions for subsequent learning activities must be very clear.

A flexible learning environment must enable students to control their learning activities. Learning about technology requires experiential learning activities which generally require significant physical resources, eg, laboratories, workshops, equipment and machinery. It is possible to develop resources to be used in the students' homes, as has been done for some Open University courses, but on a campus university this makes little sense. Using such resources in the department of design and technology was not considered to be a serious constraint on the students' control of their learning. The relevant resources for the energy unit, eg, interactive video systems and energy experiments, were freely available throughout the working day. Hence our distinction between flexible and distance learning really relates to the extent to which we have removed the administrative constraints on learning (access to relevant resources and tutorial support). The energy package currently requires facilities which are only available in our own department. Similarly tutorial support was primarily available during timetabled periods. We could have written the material in a truly distance format – ensuring there was no constraint necessitating attendance – but there seemed no reason to do so.

We decided against any attempt to establish a control group largely because it was not clear how two groups with identical prior learning experiences and comparable learning environments during the trial could be formulated. All the advice we received, as well as our own discussions, led to the conclusion that it was both more realistic and important to gauge the learning experiences and outcomes against previous years where traditional approaches had been used. This also means that we could attempt to correct anything that appeared to be going wrong with the flexible learning materials using 'traditional' approaches without worrying about undermining our evidence.

The learning materials were initially trialled with about a hundred first-year undergraduates taking foundation courses as part of their 'progress year' for degrees in industrial design and technology. The conclusions of these trials are described later.

The energy unit has been written to enable students to gain a clear understanding of energy sources, energy conversion and energy use in the home. In the future it could be easily extended to include topics like energy use in industry and energy in transport. The unit is divided into four sections:

- heat and energy
- energy and its conversion
- energy sources
- use of energy in the home.

The first student activity requires them to discuss in groups the meaning of particular technical terms and then individually to fill in 'Glossary sheet 1', which is shown in Figure 8.1.

	Definition	Units of Measurement
Mass		
Weight		
Force		
Work		
Power		
Electrical Power		
Energy		
Electrical Energy		

State the relationship between *Force* and *Work*

....

....

State the relationship between *Energy* and *Power*

....

....

Figure 8.1 *Glossary sheet 1 from the energy unit*

Figure 8.2 shows their route through the unit once this first activity has been completed. Depending on the level of difficulty encountered with the concepts associated with 'Glossary sheet 1', the students either try the diagnostic sheet or undertake some preliminary work. When the students are ready, they attempt diagnostic questions which were designed to test their understanding. After checking their answers and according to their confidence and ability, they then plan their route through the unit, entering at section 1, 2, 3 or 4 as appropriate.

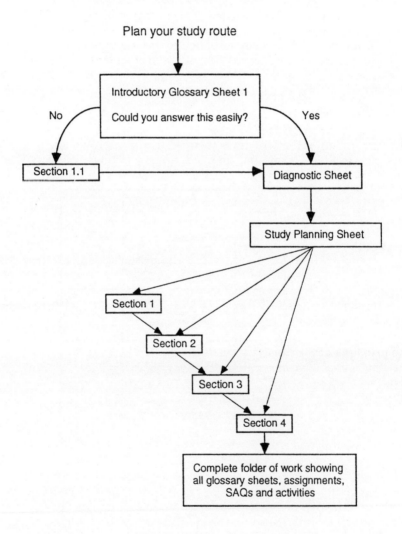

Figure 8.2 *Possible routes through the unit*

As a snapshot of the kind of activities contained within the unit, Figure 8.3 shows an abbreviated form of the beginning of section 2.

SECTION 2   **ENERGY AND ITS CONVERSION**

Objectives

By the end of section 2 you should:

- *be able to apply the principle of conservation of energy*
- *be able to calculate potential and kinetic energies for point mass and fluid systems*
- *be able to calculate the work done against resistance to motion*
- *be able to calculate energy conversion efficiencies*
- *understand heat engines and why there is a limiting efficiency*
- *understand heat pumps and refrigeration and be able to perform appropriate calculations*

2.1 Conversion of energy
You are now familiar with the definitions of work, power and energy but have not yet considered how they are converted from one form to another.

SAQ 2.1 Complete the following passage by adding one of these terms in each blank space. (You will find a duplicate passage in your folder of work that you can complete.)

kinetic energy, friction, electrical energy, thermal energy, chemical energy, power

Alison cycles home from school and uses the _____ from the food that she has eaten to provide her muscles with the _____ to ride the bike. The energy supplied is converted mainly to _____ to give ....

The principle of the conservation of energy
The principle of the conservation of energy states that ....

Figure 8.3 *The beginning of section 2 from the energy unit*

The energy unit was trialled with two different groups of undergraduates. Group A comprised approximately 50 first-year undergraduates taking a three-year degree in industrial design and technology and Group B was made up of approximately 50 first-year undergraduates taking a four-year degree in industrial design and technology with education. Some key activities associated with each section were made compulsory, eg, an analysis of the lifting action of a weight lifter on interactive videodisc at the end of section 2.

Group A was split into two classes. They had an introductory session and two two-hour timetabled sessions in alternate weeks and were not required to complete section 4. The timetabled sessions were used to distribute and support the flexible learning materials as well as being specific work time for the students. Assessment was by individual ten-minute tutorials following completion of the unit.

Group B remained as one group. They had four two-hour timetabled sessions and met each week. This group were expected to cover section 4. The timetabled sessions were used to distribute and support the flexible learning materials and included one 'impromptu' lecture (30–45 minutes) at the students' request. This group's files were taken in for assessment at the midway point as well as on completion of the unit. They were also asked to complete a questionnaire.

Discussion

It was clear that both groups had worked conscientiously and in a manner which suited their own style and pace of learning. They were also generally happy to be given the responsibility to work in this way. Students rarely worked within the department, choosing instead to make their own arrangements to meet at home or to work at some other time. Many students commented on the useful way in which the flexible learning materials provided ready-made revision notes. For these reasons the materials were popular with most students. The materials were also popular with tutors, who agreed that substantial teaching time had been saved and yet they were also confident that the quality of student learning had been maintained.

Group A had completed work which was generally of a higher standard than that of the previous year. For example, the interactive video exercise was only completed successfully by 50 per cent of the previous year's undergraduates, but with flexible learning all students had completed the exercise. Some students had used the diagnostic test in a way which had not been anticipated. They answered all the diagnostic questions by referring to small, but relevant, sections of the learning materials, ie they chose to design what they felt was a more relevant route! A few, less well motivated/organized students felt under pressure as a result of the need to take greater responsibility for their own learning.

Group B students were not as confident with the learning materials and appreciated regular feedback from tutors, even though this was often little more than a 'pat on the back'. Some requested more testing and assessment, recognizing that it might be computer-based if tutors were unable to devote more time to these activities.

Members of group B, who were asked to complete a questionnaire, identified the main advantages of flexible learning as:

● being able to work at their own pace;

- not repeating any areas of knowledge;
- generating discussion and group work;
- being able to put the appropriate time into specific topic areas;
- giving a clear indication of their own strengths and weaknesses.

They also identified the main disadvantages that they had experienced as:

- having difficulty adapting to the flexible learning approach;
- finding it hard to overcome poor motivation especially with few deadlines to meet;
- finding the learning difficult if their background was weak;
- sometimes finding it more difficult to get the necessary support.

The remaining questions required the students to give an appropriate level of response on a graded scale of 1 to 7, and evaluation of the results yielded the following observations:

- students generally felt confident about their own learning, immediately following the coursework;
- most students were able to cover most of the diagnostic questions upon completion of the coursework module;
- many students were able to miss out some of the coursework; some missed out much of the coursework;
- very little use was made of the formal planning sheet;
- most support was provided by the referenced text and by working in groups at home;
- many students felt that further support was unnecessary, but some requested an introductory lecture, tutorial and maths support.

When asked about the difficulty encountered while working through each section, there was a very wide variety of student response to the difficulty of section 1, reflecting the wide range of previous learning. Sections 2 and 3 were generally considered to be difficult by those students who worked through them.

After analysing both the questionnaire and the examination results, it was felt that the students this year had achieved a similar level of understanding of the energy topic, by flexible learning methods, to that gained the previous year by conventional teaching methods. It was also clear that the use of a flexible learning approach was of benefit to both students and teachers.

An evaluation of examination results identified small, but insignificant, changes between the student cohorts of 1992 and 1993.

Wider application across higher education

This project represents a cautious attempt to explore the possibility of using flexible learning materials to give students greater control of their learning. As such it was successful, but it cannot be concluded that such a strategy could be pursued as a general solution to the current pressures on higher education. The flexible learning materials developed here replaced the last eight hours of the 48 hours teaching on each of the two modules. They were therefore welcomed by the students as part of the consolidation and revision process. There might have been quite a different outcome if they had replaced the first eight hours teaching on the modules.

The topic chosen was also well-understood by the students to be one where there was a diverse range of prior student learning and so they could clearly see that conventional lecturing was going to be problematic. Again the result might have been quite different if the students had felt that there might be significant advantages from conventional lecturing.

It is equally clear that resourcing is important. The materials must be of high quality and those used on this project were produced with external sponsorship from British Gas to pay for the author's time. You cannot solve the problems of hard-pressed lecturing staff by expecting them to write flexible learning materials. Adopting flexible approaches to teaching and learning is, of course, quite a different matter.

In the first year very little time was gained because of the pressures of implementation and careful evaluation, but it is important to note that in the second year there are major benefits. The flexible learning materials have allowed half-hour, small group tutorials to take place in which individual progress can be monitored and discussed. This might seem a small prize for such an effort, but in these days of low staff-student ratios it adds an element of genuine quality to the later stages of the teaching of these modules.

References

Gibbs, G (1992) *Lecturing to More Students*, Oxford: The Polytechnics & Colleges Funding Council.

Norman, E W L, Riley, J L, Urry, S A and Whittaker, M (1990) *Advanced Design and Technology*, Harlow: Longman.

Chapter Nine

A Flexible Learning Scheme for a First-year Mathematics Module

Peter Lewis

Introduction

Recent changes in the British education system are increasingly affecting mathematics teaching at university level. In particular, changes in public examinations at 16 plus and, to a lesser extent, 18 plus, together with the rapid expansion in student numbers have meant that lecturers concerned with first-year undergraduate classes have a much larger and less homogeneous group of students to deal with than was previously the case.

Context

The response of the mathematical sciences department at Loughborough University of Technology to the situation has been on a number of levels:

1. A modular degree scheme introduced in 1991 is to be replaced in 1994. In the new scheme, first-year students will be able to spend more time on fundamental topics such as introductory calculus (previously implicitly assumed to be familiar to all students) and basic introductory modules are being provided in mechanics and in statistics for those students with little background in these topics.
2. Formally assessed coursework (in the form of class tests) has been introduced into a number of traditional first-year lecture courses as short-term incentives to students and also to provide feedback to staff and students on individual problem situations.
3. Various individual initiatives by members of staff have been attempted. The most radical of these is the subject of the present study. The project essentially involves the replacement of one particular first-year module, vector calculus, by a flexible learning scheme involving guided self-study

with associated class tests. The scheme was introduced in session 1992–3 with a class of 72 students. (The previous year when the module was delivered by a conventional lecture method the class size was 44. This 63 per cent expansion was indeed one of the motivations for introducing the scheme.)

The tutor had taught the topic of vector calculus for a number of years and, with a colleague, has written an introductory text book on the subject (Lewis and Ward, 1989). The subject is not usually popular with students, who have probably not yet encountered the concepts in applications such as electromagnetism or fluid mechanics. It was hoped that the new approach would stimulate more interest in the topic and give students a better grounding which would benefit them in later years.

The vector calculus module was timetabled for the second semester of the session (January to May) and followed a module in basic calculus. In the sense that most students had no previous knowledge of the subject, but all had studied the rudiments of vector algebra, the module was not perhaps the most obvious choice for a flexible learning course. However, one of the main aims in setting up the project was to offer a pilot self-study scheme in a topic where much of the teaching material was already available in text-book form and hence where lecturer preparation time could be minimized.

The intention at this stage was to gain experience of running a flexible learning scheme as an alternative to a standard lecture course, to assess student reactions to such a course and to assess the students' performance on the course in intermediate class tests and in the end-of-module examination. Longer-term intentions were:

- to find an alternative to the lecture framework which too often perhaps involves mere transmission of material from lecture notes to student notebooks with all the many possibilities for errors and misunderstandings that this process involves;
- to allow each student an alternative learning experience to be carried out largely in his/her own time and at his/her own pace. It was also felt that the experience of learning from written material would be valuable for students for their subsequent careers. Such experience is not common at undergraduate level in mathematics, particularly in the early stages of a degree course;
- for the tutor to be able to devote more of his own energies to providing individual assistance to those students experiencing difficulties and less to routine delivery of technical material;
- to use the experience gained to plan other similar courses, in particular ones where the background knowledge of the students is more varied and where a whole variety of teaching material would be necessary.

Overall the present project can be regarded as something of a staging post on the road to the development of a genuine flexible learning scheme – the present project is clearly strictly limited in its 'flexibility' and is perhaps better described as guided self-study. The project was originated and developed by the author but a number of colleagues have expressed interest and encouragement and the intention of attempting something similar themselves in the future. Clearly our particular local situation is mirrored in broad terms in many other higher education institutions and thus it is hoped that this account of one mathematics lecturer's experiences will be of interest in a wider context.

Methodology of the project

In essence the project involved the replacement of a module of 20 lectures by an integrated teaching and learning package, the components of which were as follows:

- *Main textbook.* An individual copy of the textbook referred to earlier was provided on loan to each student.
- *Other textbooks.* A few alternative textbooks on vector calculus were purchased and made available at tutorial periods and for limited borrowing by the students.
- *Study guides.* The guides were intended to help the students to find their way through the appropriate sections of the textbook. Precise reading assignments were given in each guide together with lists of which exercises were to be attempted. Important results were emphasized and those topics which could be omitted on a first reading were made clear. A deliberate attempt was made to make the study guides both user-friendly and informal.
- *Preview lectures.* A few preview lectures outlining major topics were given at appropriate intervals.
- *Tutorials.* Weekly tutorials were available for each student in two groups of about 35.
- *Class tests.* Two one-hour class tests were given in weeks five and nine of the ten-week module. The class tests were set and marked by the tutor, helped by a research student. The tests were reviewed very thoroughly in a full class session as soon as possible after being completed, with the aim of producing rapid feedback for the students.

At an introductory session the overall scheme was explained to the whole class, the objectives and logistics spelt out and all available material distributed. Students were given a suggested work timetable but it was emphasized that the only fixed points were the class test periods. Some of the students were disconcerted that an expected 20-lecture module was being replaced by an alternative scheme. Indeed three of them appeared at the course tutor's office the following day asking that the scheme be abandoned!

Thereafter, however, matters proceeded relatively smoothly. The overview lectures were reasonably well attended, the tutorials rather less so. After the first class test it was emphasized that students whose performance was demonstrably unsatisfactory would be advised to seek individual help through the tutorial system. This produced a marginal improvement in tutorial attendance.

The module straddled the university Easter vacation and the second of the class tests was deliberately timed for early in the summer term to encourage study during that vacation.

Student reaction and results

Student reaction was obtained mainly from a formal questionnaire circulated to all students near the end of the module and partly from occasional individual probings by the author. Forty-nine questionnaires were completed, a response rate of 69 per cent, which is not unreasonable given that the university now expects questionnaires to be filled in on all modules each year and a degree of overkill is undoubtedly present.

As is perhaps to be expected with any approach different from the traditional one, student reaction to the scheme as implemented was very varied. Twenty-four of the students stated that the emphasis on self-study suited them, 15 were unhappy and ten were unsure. A number of students commented on the length of time needed to work through the textbook material but several felt that this was time better spent than passively taking notes in a lecture situation. A substantial majority of the respondents stated that they did indeed enjoy being able to work at their own pace. Students who were unhappy with the scheme commented frankly that they lacked the discipline (at least at this stage of their lives) to benefit from the freedom to study when and where they chose, that they easily fell behind and would have preferred being 'dragged along', as they put it, in a lecture programme.

The written material was very favourably regarded by the great majority of the students, the textbook and in particular the study guides being extremely popular with no significant criticism being raised. The preview lectures were well-regarded by many students but some felt that their effect had been minimal. A few would have preferred consolidation lectures after they had studied the detailed material for themselves.

The students were very evenly divided as to the thoroughness of learning achieved and the speed of their learning as compared with traditional approaches. Some students, as already remarked, felt that they had learned the material thoroughly but at a substantial time cost. However, overall no very clear pattern emerged. It may be the case that the more mature, serious-minded students were well-capable of achieving an adequate understanding of the subject matter within the scheme as it was implemented. For a substantial minority of students, however, the insight, short cuts and informal alternative approaches that an experienced teacher can provide verbally are useful, if not vital. Clearly, and unsurprisingly, no single teaching and learning scheme suits all the students in a large class.

The results obtained by 66 of the 72 students in the intermediate class tests and the final examination are shown in Table 9.1. The results of the smaller 1992 class in the same module, taught by conventional lectures, are shown for comparison purposes. (The remaining six 1993 students are not considered since they were students on a new degree course which did not exist in 1991–2).

	Class size	Class average	Number of students failing	Number not attending
Test 1	66	60.8%	4	4
Test 2	66	57.6%	18	6
1993 Examination	66	48.5%	25 (38%)	0
1992 Examination	44	64.0%	10 (23%)	0

Table 9.1 *Results obtained in intermediate class tests and the final examination*

The first class test was held in week five of the module, the second in week nine (shortly after the end of the Easter vacation). Each test was one hour in duration. The end-of-module examination was one and a half hours in duration. The results of the class tests can be considered broadly acceptable, although the 36 per cent of students failing or not attending Test 2 is disappointing and there are no obvious explanations. On the other hand, 22 students did improve their performance in the second test as compared with the first. The examination performance is also contradictory – a raw average of 48.5 per cent in a fairly difficult subject is reasonable but again the 38 per cent failure rate is quite unacceptable. The comparable performance for 1992 is, at first sight, markedly better. However, it must be emphasized that the overall performance of the 1993 students was substantially worse in nearly all subjects than those of 1992 despite broadly comparable entry qualifications. The vector calculus examination average mark actually held its relative position quite well, that average being almost exactly the same as the overall class average mark in both years.

Conclusions and future plans

Any conclusions drawn must necessarily be tentative after only one trial of a teaching and learning scheme which is quite different in nature from the traditional staple fare offered to mathematics undergraduates. Undoubtedly some students enjoyed the new approach – this was clear from their verbal and written comments. Equally some students were less happy; these were not necessarily academically weak students but included some who were apparently unable to accept the self-discipline needed to carry through the scheme successfully and who, by their own admission, readily succumbed to the inevitable distractions of a residential university.

Because of the anonymity of the questionnaire it is not possible to correlate performance in the module with the degree of enjoyment but inevitably one suspects that this correlation is high. From a personal point of view the tutor has had the satisfaction of preparing written material which students have found helpful and which can certainly be reused with little or no modification. In a busy semester a lecturer has been freed from giving about 20 routine lectures, knowing that the students have access to the subject matter of the module in a much fuller, more polished form than could be provided in the lecture room. Many of the students, it is suspected, made their own summary notes of the main topics using the materials provided. This was certainly to be encouraged, both as a useful learning task in itself and because of the use of such notes for reference when the students encounter vector calculus in applications in later years of their course.

There are of course a number of incidental advantages in having course material available in a written and portable form. Two such advantages which have actually arisen are as follows:

- a partially sighted student in the class was unable to benefit fully from conventional lectures in other topics due to her inability to see visual material being presented in the lecture room. She was, however, perfectly capable of working privately through the written material for the vector calculus module and enjoyed doing so;
- any students requiring a crash course in a tool subject such as vector calculus can simply be given a copy of all the course material to read. This facility is actually being used for a mathematically-able student who is being allowed to transfer to the second year of our mathematics degree from a joint honours course in which vector calculus is not studied.

For the immediate future it is intended to offer this module in the self-study mode again for a second session. This seems sensible from nearly all points of view – the material is available, little extra costs (of time or money) will be incurred and the student intake is unlikely to be substantially different. It is planned, however, to tighten up the scheme in certain respects particularly bearing in mind those students who are less mathematically mature. Clearly, this is a difficult problem; it is simply not possible, and perhaps not even desirable, to carry out detailed checks on the individual progress of over 70 students. Increasing the frequency of class tests by a modest amount may help here but this does depend on the availability of postgraduate assistance with marking. Replacing preview lectures by a judicious combination of summary post-view lectures and worked examples classes may also help to 'drag the students along' (which is what a number of them have requested).

The biggest disappointment has been the poor attendance of students at tutorial classes. As mentioned earlier, it had been hoped, and indeed expected, that assisting with individual, or collective, difficulties on a remedial basis would be the lecturer's main activity once the scheme was underway. This however has only happened to a limited extent and then only with a small but dedicated subset of students. This problem is not of course peculiar to a self-study scheme but is a common one in a more conventional context too. The current departmental policy, under which tutorials are nominally 'compulsory' and where attendance records are kept, was not followed. Perhaps, in retrospect, this was a mistake and a tighter rein may be more appropriate. Some consideration is being given to this aspect before finalizing the scheme for its second presentation.

The major problem that is perceived by staff in higher education when considering whether or not to convert a conventional lecture course into an alternative format is the preparation time involved. Clearly this is a significant factor particularly at the outset and should not be underestimated. The author was fortunate in that a considerable amount of this effort had already been undertaken a few years earlier in writing a readable student text on the subject matter of the module. Indeed without the ready availability of this text, and the funding to allow each student to borrow an individual copy of it, it is doubtful whether the project could have been undertaken.

In general, considerable motivation is required by a lecturer with flexible learning ambitions for one or more of his or her courses. Time (above all), the level of institutional support (financial, moral and clerical) and the availability of relevant material which can be used or adapted are all factors to be taken into account. Possible gains and losses have to be carefully balanced. The lecturer whose sole aim is reduction of teaching load is unlikely to find flexible learning satisfying this aim, at least in the short term. The lecturer concerned to do his or her best for a large diverse class may find it has much more to offer.

Reference

Lewis, P E and Ward, J P (1989) *Vector Analysis for Engineers and Scientists,* Wokingham: Addison-Wesley.

Chapter Ten

A Self-guided Information Technology Profile for Student Teachers in Primary Schools

Keith Hodgkinson and Phil Wild

Primary school student teachers and information technology – problems of underskill and overload

Under the Education Reform Act of 1988 primary school teachers are now required to integrate the use of information technology (IT) into the teaching of all nine school subjects, and have to teach IT itself to all of their pupils as part of the National Curriculum for Technology. Students on one-year Post Graduate Certificate of Education (PGCE) courses for primary schools in England and Wales therefore need to learn how to use a range of computer hardware and software, and to be able to use them in their day-to-day work with children. They therefore need both to learn IT for themselves, and to have acquired sufficient confidence and competence to be able to manage and teach IT to their children in schools.

The need to learn to use IT as well as how to teach it puts students and their tutors under a considerable strain, particularly when the content of the National Curriculum subjects is changing from year to year. Primary school teachers, with whom students are placed for teaching practices and who should be able to support them in this task, themselves lack confidence and knowledge in what is for them a very new subject. Further challenges are presented by the proliferation of many different types of computers in schools, even within the same school, and the enormous variety of software available and in use.

Student teachers begin their training with a very wide range of expertise in IT, some lacking any experience and crucially showing all the symptoms of technophobia (Blackmore *et al.*, 1992). By using non-didactic and experiential pedagogics, teacher training courses have nevertheless been able to raise student confidence and competence at all levels of expertise within the short time available (Wild and Hodgkinson, 1992). In the education department at Loughborough, student development in IT is effectively enhanced and monitored through a flexible, individualized personal learning plan (PLP), an eight-page A5 leaflet which records IT use in the department and in schools. This is formally assessed as a coursework assignment which also functions as an effective profile of student achievement.

A more recent investigation (Hodgkinson and Wild, 1994) showed that, however well taught on courses within the higher education institution, students still experienced great difficulty in applying their IT skills in their teaching in schools. The problem seemed to be that a significant number of class teachers were not giving students the support and encouragement they needed in order for them to be able to plan and deliver IT in their teaching. This gap between the achievements of students on campus and the capacity to apply learning while on placement is perhaps typical of off-site experience in higher education. But in the case of trainee teachers the problem is urgent because, as a consequence of the government's plans for the reform of teacher training, most or all of student learning will have to take place in the schools themselves where, as we know already, the levels of IT expertise and confidence are low.

Context

At Loughborough the primary course is fortunate in being well-resourced for IT, with workstations in all teaching rooms as well as a fully equipped open learning centre for IT. All students receive an immediate induction into IT in the first week of the course. Flexible teaching is by structured exercises for small groups, allowing for individual attention particularly for those starting off at low confidence levels.

Targets for children's use of IT in the classroom are set by the National Curriculum documentation and students are encouraged to link their methods work with this framework. The five strands or applications of IT in education are defined (NCET,1991) as:

1. Communicating information
2. Handling information
3. Modelling
4. Measurement and control
5. Applications and effects.

Each strand has its own required competences for pupils, who must be placed on one of six levels of attainment for each, compounded for one IT level overall. Each of the five strands should be applied across the nine subjects. The complexity involved in mapping and monitoring the achievements of each pupil in this nexus can easily be imagined.

Approximately half of the 36-week course is spent in schools, including two block teaching practices of four and six weeks during which the students are responsible for planning and teaching the whole curriculum for one class of children aged 7–11.

Aims of the project

The main general aim of the project was to improve significantly the extent of student application of IT in their teaching placements in schools, particularly during their final teaching practice in the summer term. The project was intended to modify and improve on the established PLP for IT. The new flexible learning plan (FLP) would be more user-friendly with a more professional layout; it would also be more spacious and more demanding. It would require students to engage in discussion with the class teachers and, crucially, would require the teacher(s) to countersign the final record, thus involving them personally in the whole process.

A secondary aim was to widen the scope of the original PLP to include a record of personal IT management skills developed by each student. These include:

formatting disks
creating and deleting files
copying disks
setting up a workstation
carrying out a class/school IT audit.

The last task could of course prove to be extremely useful for the school itself – a major selling point when asking teachers to give more help than they offer at present. More personal management use might be encouraged by asking them to record their use of IT for designing lesson preparation/plans, and for making class worksheets and handouts.

The redesign process

An initial review of the problem suggested that the current instrument, the PLP, provided such consistent results and was so easy to use and to administer that to make really radical changes or to reject it altogether would be to throw out the baby with the bath water. The revised booklet would continue to be multi-functional, of real value to students, practical for assessment purposes and yet effective in engaging students' class teachers.

A first revision was trialled on a small group of students on the final (summer) teaching practice. The effectiveness of the FLP pilot could then be assessed by directly comparing the FLP scores with those scores achieved by students in the past, on their PLPs and on end-of-course questionnaires. No experimental/control group design was envisaged, however, as there were too many other variables (students, schools, ages of children, class teachers) for valid analysis for the group size (such are the difficulties of educational research!).

The final process was to be as follows:

- review/analysis of the old-style PLPs;
- first draft design of the new FLP;
- pilot use in the summer term;

- redesign, full use from October;
- student use over one year, assessed in July.

The first draft led to improved layout with more space for student records and additional material on the various strands of IT use derived from national documentation (DES, 1989; NCET, 1991). The result was a compilation of personal and classroom management skills, put in simple, non-technical language. Students were also asked to record the type of computer used in order to build up a detailed personal profile of their achievement over the year.

Next came the 'School IT audit'. Something short but incisive was needed, requiring students to ask questions on their preliminary (serial) visits to schools and thus forcing them to make advanced preparations for hardware and software variety and which would necessarily involve the teachers, we hoped, at the same time.

Pilot results

In May, a week before the placement began, volunteers were invited to try out the new FLP. They were thus a self-selected group, and therefore probably among the more confident and enthusiastic IT learners. Six out of 60 were involved, a 10 per cent sample. One more helpful student handed in both the old and the new profile and this enabled us to make a very useful comparison. Tutors also had brief discussions with individuals and this provided further information.

All six of the completed trial FLPs were satisfactory on all of the main counts: students found them easy to complete and user-friendly, and their records were full, easy to read and interpret and provided almost as much information as the old PLPs. The last page, on 'Personal management skills' and 'School IT audit' proved to be highly successful. They seemed to have encouraged students to think about far more than just running software programmes for children, and they certainly involved them in making their own assessments of their schools' IT provision. To quote one response: 'The teachers at R...H... do not use computers. Children are on a rota system and go to the IT room about once a term'. Five of the six named the IT coordinator and all had recorded all types of computer in use. This information was to prove most helpful in a future response to students' needs in schools.

The FLPs were marked for formal assessment purposes. The pilot students gained 70–80 per cent, significantly higher than the average for the whole group but no conclusions could be drawn from this other than that the process of assessment was as straightforward as before and gave positive results.

In discussion the pilot group said that they would advise combining the best features of the old and new plans. Thus although the space allowance on the FLP was adequate, the new design had omitted a free blank page on which several of the more interested students had written open-ended 'further comments'. These comments had been of high quality, showing mature reflection and great sophistication. The extra space undoubtedly encouraged the more committed students to demonstrate and develop their IT capability, so it was decided to incorporate this feature in the new FLP.

The pilot results also show a need for two more categories of IT use: 'music' on teaching use and 'writing assignments' for the personal management section.

At a late stage in the redesign, we received further guidance from the National Council for Educational Technology on the requirements for children's learning across all strands of IT use. We decided, somewhat reluctantly, to include a double-page spread incorporating this new profile, and requiring students to tick each use through the year. This extra task, set late and without consultation with the student body, was perceived to be an artificial exercise, imposed by outsiders and unrelated to primary classroom reality. It will not be included in future versions.

The final eight-page A4 version, the flexible learning plan, was produced in September and was submitted to each of the next year's students in October.

Discussion and future development

With the exception noted above, the new FLP seemed to be a significant improvement on the old, very limited version. It allowed more space for the better students to expand on their experiences, it provided more structured guidance on how they should manage their IT use in schools, and it included more categories of such use in line with National Curriculum guidelines.

For the following year it was decided to make a number of minor amendments:

- a revised Introduction on page 1 placing the task within the wider context of students' career development;
- extra space on the final pages: a blank section for further comments plus a new section on students' future needs in IT teaching. These pages were intended to promote further reflection on their current development and forward planning for in-service education.

Student experience of the new plan has been monitored throughout the year. Early results show that students are happy with most features, reflecting the experiences with the pilot version. The plan is already giving a much more detailed picture of their management of IT in the classroom and provides a useful profile of individual student development. In one important respect, however, the plan has serious shortcomings. Teacher input is still minimal, possibly because it is limited to a signature only; we now need to consider building in a requirement for a more positive contribution by the teachers themselves. This will probably consist of a formative assessment of students' IT work linked to the school's formal report on the teaching practice as a whole.

In the light of closer partnership between schools and university trainers this further development of the FLP must now be a collaborative enterprise by tutors and class teachers. University tutors and researchers, however, will still retain the primary responsibility for innovative developments in educational practice. We must seek ways in which to force the discussion between the partners – students and teachers – about the process of learning the use of IT in schools. The new plan has now been placed at the crux of the 'sandwich' structure of teacher education – an exciting position to be in, but an uncomfortable one.

References

Blackmore, M, Stanley, N, Coles, D, Hodgkinson, K, Taylor, C and Vaughan, G (1992) 'A preliminary view of students' information technology experience across UK initial teacher training institutions', *Journal of Information Technology in Teacher Education*, 1, 2, 241–54.

DES (1989) *Information Technology in Initial Teacher Training (The Trotter Report)* London: HMSO.

Hodgkinson, K and Wild, P (1994) 'Tracking the development of student IT capability: IT in the primary PGCE over three years', *Journal of Information Technology in Teacher Education*, 3, 1, 101–14.

NCET (1991) *Focus on IT: IT in the National Curriculum*, Coventry: National Council for Educational Technology.

Wild, P and Hodgkinson, K (1992) 'IT capability in primary initial teacher training', *Journal of Computer Assisted Learning*, 8, 79–89.

Chapter Eleven

A Business School Approach to Flexibility in Course Provision

Alison Smith

The Business School approach to flexibility in course provision is concentrated initially upon post-experience management education. This chapter outlines recent developments in management education which have brought about the need for a more flexible focus, explains why the Loughborough University Business School is concentrating effort upon its post-experience provision, and outlines both the progress that has been made and the future direction.

Why flexible approaches to course provision?

Increased undergraduate student numbers are driving the development of innovation in teaching and learning across the range of university departments. Business education, like the majority of subject specialisms, is no exception to the increasing demands placed upon the same teaching resource. Coping with the pressure of increased student numbers is only one facet of the current working environment of those in higher education. Alongside these resource demands is the equally important need to develop and maintain a strong research profile. Balancing these two requirements to achieve quality outputs in both areas necessitates some deft juggling and it is clear that teaching innovation is paramount to the solution of some of the teaching problems. It is also becoming apparent that new approaches to teaching may offer research opportunities.

Management education: the context for flexibility

The management education market has experienced significant change within the last few years. In addition to increasing undergraduate numbers, the later 1980s saw the promotion of increased provision for the postgraduate and post-experience market. The Handy (1987) and Constable and McCormack (1987) reports revealed the lack of management training available in this country in comparison with our overseas competitors and recommended the development of courses to meet this particular need. The arrival on the scene of the Management Charter Initiative (MCI), an employer-led group, promoted the development of management standards of competence and qualifications based on demonstrable ability to perform the management job.

The increased demand for management training in the UK experienced during the latter half of the 1980s may be attributed to these events. However, the economic recession which followed depleted training budgets if not demand. In response to the continuing need for post-experience and postgraduate management training set alongside the budgetary constraints, more flexible provision must be devised to enable managers to continue their development. Inevitably, this means less time in the classroom and more time devoted to other forms of learning and to exploiting and supporting the learning opportunities provided in the management role.

The Business School strategy

The Business School at Loughborough University of Technology is a well-established provider of postgraduate and post-experience education. The latter has typically taken the form of tailored short courses. In order to continue to meet the needs of corporate clients within the context of the changes outlined above, it has been recognized that new forms of delivery must be devised. Part of the Business School strategy is to develop its post-experience portfolio through innovative provision of learning opportunities and off-campus support for courses designed for corporate clients. The major outcomes of this initiative will be satisfaction of management training needs of clients and improved access to postgraduate programmes for experienced managers. It is envisaged that this latter outcome in particular will also help the School to maintain and develop its research profile.

How and where to begin?

The following outlines the origins of the project and describes the initial progress that has been made.

The School has taken a decision to begin its work in this area by targeting its new accredited professional programmes in management which have been designed to meet MCI requirements for competence-based training. These are currently offered to single companies and provide them with tailored training which offers a qualification and access to postgraduate study. Through these courses, the School maintains strong links with industry which inform undergraduate teaching and help maintain a 'real world' focus.

The Business School flexible learning project is thus aimed initially at this clearly defined area of management education with a view to extending the benefits to other areas and other student groups as appropriate. The objective is to develop off-campus support for part-time 'manager-students' participating in the professional programmes which involve modular, block attendance courses at the university. These students' needs are often specialized and the outcomes of their study are required to be highly visible within the company. Consequently, the Business School needs to develop a high degree of customer focus. The needs and expectations of these managers are frequently different from those of the traditional university student because of their broad experience, clearly defined requirements and limited time (see Chapter 4 for more detail). As students they can be demanding and critical customers but providing for their needs can be seen as a standard for the range of Business School provision.

More customer-focused delivery may involve distance learning and/or multimedia packages for content delivery. It may also involve exploring and developing support networks in order to achieve an enjoyable learning experience and demonstrable company benefits as well as good pass marks.

It is not the Business School's intention to provide courses totally by distance learning, rather it is to enhance current delivery strategies and to improve the learning experience. This means looking at the student's situation, needs and the company expectations, before designing accordingly. It means starting from where they are rather than from what we can do. In essence, the School is putting into practice the principles it teaches.

The nature and needs of companies and their students

Company students differ in many respects from the majority of the student population. In most cases they are older than the average undergraduate and are likely to have only the opportunity of part-time study. They may be returning to learning after a considerable time; they may not have previously followed an academic course of study; they have full-time jobs and may also have family responsibilities. They are unlike the typical undergraduate who usually arrives 'in learning mode' and with very little else to tax the mind other than developing a sense of individual responsibility.

Companies in the 1990s which support training for their staff are looking for cost-effective means. There is therefore a need to continue to offer high quality management education and to look for new forms of delivery which companies can afford. Recent research (Smith, 1993) revealed that companies are increasingly attracted to distance learning as it is seen by the sponsor as cost-effective. It does, however, require commitment and self-sufficiency and may not be appropriate as the total learning medium for students who need considerable support.

Business School response

Accredited training within a supportive structure is the proposed solution to these problems. The benefits to corporate sponsors are felt to be improved efficiency of the management development process and reduction of costs associated with attendance based courses such as time, accommodation and travel. For students, learning strategies will be tailored more effectively to the needs of the mature, part-time post-experience individual who needs to apply skills rapidly and tangibly.

The specific products which the project seeks to develop are flexible learning packages which will be designed, piloted and evaluated with the target student groups. To ensure that this work is founded upon sound academic principles and that it meets the requirements of our corporate customers (both students and their sponsors), investigations and projects are being undertaken as follows:

- a full literature survey of open learning;
- assessment of student needs;
- the design of flexible learning packages.

The first pilot package has required the transformation of an academic paper into a self-learning package to be completed by students as pre-reading material. This package is shortly to be sent to students and it will be evaluated by comparison with earlier cohorts of students who experienced the paper in its original form as pre-course reading and associated preparatory work.

In the future, there will be collaboration with lecturers to design, deliver and evaluate other learning methodologies to be used both during the course and off-campus. Currently an overview of best practice is being developed through secondary data search, attending academic and practitioner conferences and gathering examples of innovative concepts within this university, within other higher education institutions and within organizations. The learning from this experience will be consolidated, piloted further with the professional programmes students and transferred as appropriate to other courses.

An overview of the findings from the initial research into student needs is provided below.

Issues in flexible learning: students and clients

The following issues have emerged, both from continuing informal discussion with clients and from research with current students. These issues have an important bearing upon project development.

Students

Our target group of students has, in the past, completed study via short courses supported by distance learning in the form of guided reading. A survey of a recently graduated group has revealed the following.

Standardization of distance learning needs to be considered. The volume of reading in many modules was daunting and the guidance variable. Similarly there was variation in the degree of difficulty in the reading material, both in content and style. Individual lecturers have varied in their approach to the guided reading between those who instructed students to read a number of chapters and those who advised on what the students should be looking for in the reading or what they should be able to do, having read.

Students volunteered other support areas where they had encountered problems. These were largely concerned with their positions as full-time managers, mature students and location across the country (see Chapter 4 for a full review). Specifically they have encountered problems with library access, obtaining and returning books, recall problems and the inability to use the library's short loan facility. They could use other university libraries, but as reading rooms only, and for those located in the remoter areas of the UK this was not an option.

Isolation from their fellow students and from the university itself has caused problems when learning at a distance. Despite building relation-ships during the taught periods, it has been difficult to maintain these when back at work. Some students were located in the same geographical area and some in the company's head office. The former fared better in terms of peer support and the latter group had access to better company support. Those working in field locations were isolated. Access to lecturers was also not easy. Although the students felt lecturers were willing to see them and talk to them by telephone, the logistical aspects of making this happen were problematic.

Students also felt that the taught elements of the course were highly concentrated with little time for reflection and questioning. The comment was made that the short course elements were like having quarts in pint pots and, since the students returned to work immediately after each 'injec-tion', their assimilation of the input was again carried out in isolation.

The unique nature of company culture and working practices means that initiatives which would benefit these particular company students would be of little benefit elsewhere. For example, the provision of cassette tapes was identified by a number of the students as a useful aid, but only for those who spent a considerable amount of work time travelling by car. A range of learning material may thus need to be provided for a company, and other companies may have a completely different need depending upon the nature of the industry, the student-managers' roles and the company culture. Clearly, the decision to invest in cassettes, either as general support material or designed specifically for a company, cannot be taken without further company-by-company research into potential use.

The students felt that mentoring, done well, is very valuable and that this is a key area for the future. In their experience the quality of the mentoring had been variable.

Clients
The companies are engaging internally upon more flexible approaches to training. While undoubtedly driven by increased cost-consciousness,

training and management development managers are looking to develop staff by more self-directed means. The emphasis is upon personal responsibility with managers driving the fulfilment of their own development needs. The growth of interest in personal development plans, empowerment, learning cultures and the learning organization (Pedler *et al.*, 1991) is a reflection of this growing trend towards managers driving their own development.

There is reduced enthusiasm for traditional taught courses since it is felt they require less commitment from the participants – merely the ability to attend. While it is recognized that some learning, and some learners, will always require an element of classroom teaching, outcomes of the learning are receiving greater emphasis.

Companies are developing learning approaches, as distinct from teaching approaches. This is evidenced in such initiatives as project-based learning, action learning groups, networks and training for work competence. 'DIY learning' is gaining ground upon learning which is designed, delivered and installed by experts. Providers are now being asked to design learning approaches which the company undertakes in-house with the students.

There is increased use of self-directed learning packages, both multimedia and text-based, where participants set their own agendas and time for learning. In all of these, the payback to the sponsor is felt to be more evident and the immediate financial cost less.

Training budgets within companies remain very restricted but the desire to train (or to facilitate learning) is still in evidence. This situation demands that both providers and sponsors initiate more creative means of development, involving companies as joint providers (Smith, 1993). This has implications for assessment and universities are already being asked to accredit internal company provision with some form of higher education certification. While this chapter is not the place to debate what is a large and separate issue, it is worth noting the potential which National Vocational Qualifications offer for developing this kind of joint approach.

The groundwork covered during this stage of the study has raised a number of issues which have enabled an agenda to be devised for the next stage. A new group of company students, with equally diverse problems and from similarly different locations will begin their programme in October 1995. Needs analysis for this group will entail detailed research into their attitudes towards flexible approaches, their ability to handle flexible learning, their off-site facilities and their support needs. Analysis of the work environment and of the sponsor's motivation in adopting a flexible approach will also be carefully considered.

Conclusion

The Business School sees this as an ongoing project which will develop through close monitoring and evaluation of strategies with different groups. The progress made in understanding the flexible learning context has confirmed our belief that the direction we are following is a valid and necessary one, albeit far from straightforward in practice. The initiative we have embarked upon here will, we feel, enable us to develop a much stronger service culture which will impact very positively upon the full range of course provision and the ongoing development of teaching quality within the Business School.

Acknowledgement

The Business School would like to acknowledge support for research into flexible learning from the Foundation for Management Education (FME) which has provided funds for a three-year study.

References

Constable, J and McCormack, R (1987) *The Making of British Managers*, London: BIM/CBI.
Handy, C (1987) *The Making of Managers*, London: MSC/NEDO/BIM.
Pedler, M, Burgoyne, J and Boydell, T (1991) *The Learning Company: A strategy for sustainable development*, Maidenhead: McGraw-Hill.
Smith, A J (1993) *Corporate Sponsorship of MBAs*, Loughborough University Business School Research Series, Paper 1993:7.
Smith, A J (1993) 'The controversial MBA', *Training Tomorrow*, October, 23–5.

Chapter Twelve

A Distance Learning Programme for Design Engineers

Ian Wright

Introduction

The Engineering Design Institute at Loughborough University of Technology offers a successful MSc programme in engineering design. Since the course started in 1991, it has attracted 30 full-time students per year and has built up a strong part-time population from students who are employed in industry. The most important aspect of the course that influences its ability to attract employed engineers is its structure, which is based upon one-week modules. The course consists of ten of these plus a major design project. Each module is self-contained, and covers a particular topic.

Although the course is successful in attracting students, a large untapped market exists that is not accessed by the current provision. This market consists of potential part-time students who cannot get the necessary periods away from their company. These students frequently enquire if a distance learning option is available.

Student profile and implications

Establishing a typical student profile was an essential step in planning the distance learning programme. From a knowledge about students who had expressed interest in a distance learning option, it was observed that their age distribution and employment sector were indistinguishable from part-time students currently registered on the course. On this basis, it was reasonable to construct the profile from a survey of existing students. This survey was based upon a sample of 50 students which, in November 1992, represented approximately 80 per cent of the total student population.

The survey shows that the mean age is 35 years. With the students 'graduating' from either a first degree or HND course in their early to mid-20s, this means that a typical student will have had no formal education over the past ten years. Experience with these students on the traditional course indicates that, although their motivation is higher than the typical 25-year-old full-time student, they have a higher level of doubt about their ability to cope with the learning environment. This is reflected in a heightened need for approval and encouragement from the tutor, a factor that has obvious support implications in a distance learning environment. Most of these students were involved with the design of products which require multi-disciplinary skills, and gained promotion to project management at between 27 and 35 years of age.

Structure of the distance learning programme

It was decided to produce the distance learning package in the form of a course guide and associated source text. Other, more 'exciting' options were considered and rejected on the basis of educational requirement and cost. However, the case for the inclusion of an audiotape was seen as an acceptable addition to text for the 'Setting objectives' package. Although most students readily understand the basic principles, they frequently find it difficult to imagine how a particular technique could be introduced into their company. This is not because the techniques are difficult to use, but because the information required is not readily available. However, the gathering and collation of this information does not require any special skills, but merely hard work and a methodological approach. This requires encouragement, and audiotapes can provide this effectively.

Although the course guide forms the organizational core of the learning package, the course text contains the bulk of the basic information to be presented to the student. The design methodologies lectures on the masters course had, for some years, required Nigel Cross's book *Engineering Design Methods* (Cross, 1991) to be essential reading, and this was chosen as the course text for the distance learning programme. Regardless of its suitability as the course text, Cross's book was not written to meet the needs of the distance learner. The major shortcomings in this respect are: (a) an absence of exercises for the student to undertake; (b) examples and case studies which either present simple products in a detailed way or complicated examples in an over-simplified way, thereby not preparing the student for real problems; and (c) omitting (for clarity and/or brevity) a number of issues essential for the practitioner.

With the previous points in mind, the objectives for the course guide can be defined as follows:

● provide a structure to the student's reading in order to package information into manageable packets and set objectives for each packet;
● reinforce learning with detailed worked examples;
● help the student to question the advantages and limitations of the methods;

- assist the student to apply the techniques to real problems in his/her organization by means of assignments;
- provide additional core learning material where it is considered that the course text is inadequate;
- provide motivation and encouragement by means of varied learning techniques, visual and written style, audio interviews, and links into personal tutor support.

It was decided that the course guide should become the repository for all of the student's personal notes, answers to self-assessment questions (SAQs), and assignment solutions undertaken as part of the programme of study. This results in the student having a single source of reference when revising for formal examination, and the student's personal tutor being able to check the student's progress through answers to SAQs.

Coherent package design

Good graphic design is imperative in a distance learning package. Visual entities other than text and contextual diagrams are required to act as signposts, identifiers and milestone indicators, in addition to their equally important role of providing stimulation. These 'design' aspects include the layout of text blocks to accentuate issues and activities, the use of 'page turning' to signify the start or finish of an activity, the appropriate juxtaposition of text and graphics, and the use of icons to flag different types of activity. These aspects of graphic design, and an imaginative use of the written word, are necessary to make the students feel that they are interacting with their tutor even when studying alone. A description of the design and production processes used in the preparation of the package is shown in Figure 12.1. The following sections provide an overview of the major project phases identified in the figure.

Define objectives
In providing objectives for the package, it is temptingly easier to state teaching objectives presented in the form of a syllabus rather than to specify learner objectives. However, learner objectives provide a much more precise description of output. The learner objectives for the 'Setting objectives' package are as follows:

Students will be able to:
- determine the objectives and constraints for the design of an engineering product;
- utilize methods to establish and/or improve communication between engineers when determining objectives and constraints;
- produce a detailed product design specification;
- critically and constructively assess a product design specification;
- apply the principles and techniques to any market requirement in any engineering discipline;

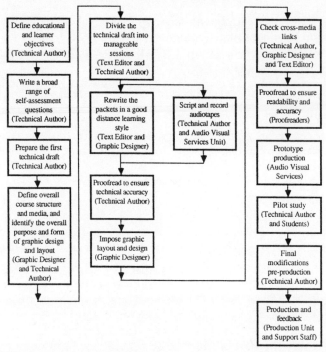

Figure 12.1 *The design and production processes used in the preparation of the distance learning package*

● assign weightings to objectives in order to signify their relative importance.

Self-assessment questions (SAQs)

If authors can define what the student will be able to do as a result of completing the course, they can also write questions to test if the student has acquired the prescribed knowledge, skills, etc. With the learner objectives and the SAQs established, the specification for the technical draft is firmly in place.

Preparation of technical draft

In an ideal world, the teacher would go to the filing cabinet and retrieve a complete, legible set of notes ready to convert into distance learning format. This was not the case with the 'Setting objectives' package. Like most lecturers, this technical author's lecture material is a mixture of good handouts, overhead transparencies requiring verbal explanation, a few slides, notes on backs of envelopes, and 50 per cent in memory. The task of producing a full set of good quality lecture notes is something that most lecturers only dream of as they are about to start the course each year. However, this is exactly what *must* be done before work on the distance learning package can start. For most lecturers, the task is mammoth. Although the author had the advantage of having a course text, the preparation of technical material for the course guide was still a substantial task.

Definition of structure and media
If all of the technical draft is available, this phase is usually straightforward. Because all the draft was not available, mistakes were made which had to be put right later. In particular, the later addition of case studies revealed the useful potential of audiotapes as an additional supporting medium. This relatively late decision caused a major rewrite of the package to be undertaken.

Subdivision into sessions
This is an important phase in the planning of a distance learning package. A student using the package will benefit from knowing how long each part of the course is likely to take to complete, and the student is less likely to feel dispirited than if he/she is still battling through a session four or five hours after starting. One of the important keys to distance learning is rewarding effort, and the completion of a session within a reasonable and predicted time period will encourage the student to go further.

Rewriting for distance learning
Although some technical authors will wish to undertake the task of adapting their own material to a distance learning form, it is unreasonable to expect them to have this particular skill. For this project, the task was completed jointly by the technical author and an off-campus consultancy specializing in this type of work and graphic design.

Audiotape preparation
The scripting of audiotapes is not an automatic skill for academics. As an over-simplification, two options are available: (a) tape conversations can be fully scripted in which case there is a danger that they sound 'wooden', or (b) they can be 'off-the-cuff' interviews, with the result that the interviewee never says what you expect. In practice, the best solution is to go for (a) with sufficient practice to allow everyone to feel relaxed.

Proofing technical accuracy
With all of this diverse professional input to the learning package, there is a risk that the end result will be a wonder of graphic design, media application, and dynamic authorship, which will no longer meet the stated learner objectives. Proofreading by the technical author is an essential part of the verification process.

Graphic design and layout
It is far from certain that graphic designers will have sufficient or indeed

any experience of distance learning to enable them to propose appropriate page layout and graphic design elements. Again, the technical author needs to be involved to provide input to the process.

Checking cross-media links
This phase is concerned with ensuring that referrals from one medium to another (eg, course guide to course text, course guide to audiotape and vice versa) are accurate. This may *seem* trivial to the uninitiated.

Full proofread
When the final draft becomes available, full proofreading can be undertaken. This should be done by people who have had no previous involvement with the preparation of course material. This ensures that preconceived ideas about integrity are not carried into the proofreading phase.

Prototype production
The purpose of prototype production is to prepare a small number of packages for piloting. The prototypes must be identical, or identical in all important aspects, to the proposed final product.

A decision had been made earlier to produce double-sided stationery onto which the text of the course guide could be laser printed. The availability of this stationery, plus printed front covers meant that the prototypes were, in fact, identical to the proposed final product. Prototype course guides were wire-bound and shrink-wrapped together with a course text and audiotape. Ten prototype packages were produced.

Pilot study
Five prototype packages were sent to students who had previously completed the design methodologies module as part-time students. The purpose was to attempt to establish if these students felt that the package was an improvement on the traditional teaching methods that they had experienced. Students were asked to undertake all of the SAQs and assignment exercises, and to complete an enclosed questionnaire. The remaining prototype packages were completed by employed engineers who were not students on the postgraduate MSc course. These engineers all had the academic qualifications necessary for course entry.

Final modifications
Encouragingly, the piloting of the package did not identify a need for major modifications. All of the students who had previously studied the material by traditional means, considered that the package would have:

● improved their understanding of principles and applications;
● provided a good 'lead-in' if supplied as pre-course reading;

● provided a much improved set of notes for revision purposes.

The users of the remaining prototype packages found them to be:

● conveniently paced and segmented;
● encouraging and motivating;
● interesting to use.

The only criticism to be levelled against the package by these five users was that the package did not contain a sufficiently wide spread of all of the methodologies used in industry. However, this was acceptable because the package would eventually form only one part of a series of packages covering a much wider span of methodologies.

Production and feedback

One of the major advantages of the chosen method of production is that justifiable criticism of the product in service, or the needs of developments in the field of study, can be readily incorporated in subsequent versions without having to scrap large volumes of printed stock.

Outcomes

In November 1993, the package was adopted as standard teaching material on the engineering design methodologies module of the MSc course. Part-time and full-time students were provided with the package three weeks prior to the start of the university-based module with instructions to complete all of the SAQs and assignments by the start date. As might be expected, the response was mixed, but out of 44 students (30 full-time and 14 part-time) only four (all full-time) had failed to make an acceptable effort. The response by the students to the material was overwhelmingly supportive. Interpreting assignment requirements was the only pre-module support requested. As expected, part-time students required more support than full-time students in this respect.

From the teachers' point of view, use of the package ensured that attendees started the module with a similar level of pre-knowledge, hence overcoming a problem that had caused severe difficulties in previous years. The practical experience gained by the students in undertaking assignments also prepared them for the group work undertaken within the module. The improvement here was so large that lecturing staff were unprepared for the increased performance and work rate, and had to develop more advanced project work as the module progressed.

At present, only 50 per cent of the subject matter taught on the module is covered by the package. Progress is being made towards the preparation of a further package for the remainder, and it is intended that the entire module will be available in a distance learning format by the 1995/6 academic year.

Reference

Cross, N (1991) *Engineering Design Methods*, Chichester: John Wiley.

Chapter Thirteen

Flexible Learning in English

Brian Jarvis

Introduction

Lecturers in English departments in higher education in Britain had been dedicated to the principles of adaptability in teaching practice and sensitivity to the needs of individual students for some time before the appearance of the term 'flexible learning'. The commitment has always been there, but, regrettably, particularly over the last decade and a half, the resources necessary to realize these principles have often been missing. In this context, the entirely appropriate questions which our profession will want answered are: 'What does "flexible learning" mean to, and what can it do for, lecturers in English?' 'Are we faced by anything more than a new vocabulary, a series of "buzz phrases", with which to articulate goals which it is increasingly difficult to achieve?' 'Is "flexible learning" merely a voguish rhetoric which distracts from deteriorating conditions in higher education?' The aim of this chapter is to suggest that while a certain amount of scepticism about flexible learning is appropriate, there are also pressing pragmatic and pedagogic reasons to give serious consideration to the range of initiatives currently being developed under this generic heading. This chapter will begin by outlining these reasons before going on to suggest certain means of responding to current conditions, detailing their benefits and potential pitfalls.

Context

Teaching in higher education in the 1990s, one is confronted by numerous intra- and extra-institutional pressures which impact upon our work experience and the learning experience of our students and seem almost certain to intensify during the foreseeable future. The national squeeze on resources increasingly feels like a stranglehold and concurrently many institutions are having to come to terms with critical changes to funding procedures, the instigation of widespread teaching assessment, the transition to modularization and semesterization and the rise of student/staff ratios, something which is particularly acute in English departments.

In this context, it is imperative to stave off the prospect of a degree in English becoming an increasingly passive learning experience in ever-larger and more anonymous groups, that we consider the efficacy of new teaching techniques designed to facilitate a greater amount of participation by students in their own education. The past few years has witnessed a burgeoning of forums designed to disseminate information enabling lecturers to negotiate the difficulties associated with rapidly changing conditions by learning from each others' experiences.

An affirmative pedagogical case can be advanced in favour of flexible learning strategies. The transition which has been taking place since the late 1960s within our discipline, the various debates over what should constitute 'English' at undergraduate level (discussion about the canon and works by marginalized writers), ought to be accompanied by a thorough consideration of the teaching practices associated with traditional definitions of the subject. These recent challenges issued to definitions of the discipline have been accompanied by a shift in secondary education towards continuous assessment and project work. This shift has equipped the prospective English undergraduate with new skills and encouraged different expectations about university learning, both of which can be met by flexible learning initiatives. A move beyond what may be called the 'jug method of learning' – whereby the teacher, presumed to be the fountain of all wisdom, pours knowledge into the empty vessel that is the mind of the undergraduate student – is not only in accordance with recent developments in the discipline and in GCSE courses; it can also foster that independence and initiative, that willingness to take responsibility for one's own learning, which are the prerequisite skills for postgraduate study.

Process and outcomes

In *The Dream Songs* the American poet John Berryman recalls that, as a boy, his mother would regularly reprimand him for suggesting that he was bored: 'Ever to confess you're bored/ means you have no/ Inner Resources' (Berryman, 1972). Irrespective of the 'inner resources' of our students, lecturers have a responsibility to avoid that monotony and predictability which stifle the possibilities of learning. Obviously, flexible learning is nowhere near to being a definitive solution to the perennial problem of motivating students who are bored and unreceptive, but it can go some way towards generating that variety at both the micro-level of a particular seminar and the macro-level of a module or entire degree programme which can promote high levels of interest and interaction.

Self-managed learning in small groups

Small-group learning is the most frequently deployed form of flexible teaching strategy in the seminar situation. Where appropriate it can also be an effective substitute for the 'formal' one-hour lecture. The provision of information which is usually delivered orally in a worksheet format can establish the basis for a more active participation by students in the acquisition of knowledge than the largely passive process of note-taking.

Small-group seminars tend to be most productive when students are divided into groups of between four and six members and each is given a *choice of task and role*. Thus, rather than restricting a group to an agenda which is determined entirely by the lecturer – asking only questions to which s/he already has *the* answer – students can be required to arrive at the seminar with questions of their own in certain general categories ('thematics', 'critical passages' and 'key words', 'issues of form', the relevance of 'biographical information' and 'historical context') and to assume roles such as the member responsible for 'questions', 'answers', 'arbitration' and 'summarizing'. Typically, the role of the lecturer during these sessions will evolve in the course of the year and in conjunction with developments in group dynamics. Initially, a far greater degree of supervision may be necessary, but as students grow familiar with this type of learning small groups can become almost entirely self-managed.

Problems with this approach and solutions

There are two major difficulties associated with small-group work, both of which illustrate the fact that, at least to begin with, the process of encouraging students to teach themselves in certain areas makes as many demands upon the lecturer, in terms of planning and coordination, as do more traditional forms of teaching. First, there is the problem of guaranteeing the relevance of discussion during these sessions. One means by which this can be negotiated is through the provision of worksheets as the basis for small-group discussion. Such documents need to maintain an appropriate balance in their composition between the specificity which is required to keep colloquy 'on the right lines', without being so rigid as to stifle the possibility of student initiative. Preferably they ought to be distributed in advance of a seminar meeting. Second, lecturers can encounter the obstacle of student expectation. Changes can be met with scepticism and some resistance by students who, learning in ever-larger groups, may assume that a seminar is simply an extension of the lecture and an opportunity to hone their skills as transcribers. This obstacle is best overcome by a thorough briefing of students at the beginning of a course and in the documents which they have access to when taking decisions about course enrolment.

The purpose of small-group work needs to be explained fully to convince the sceptical that rather than an abdication of responsibility by the lecturer, it can provide a good opportunity for them to play a more active part in their education. It can develop skills in communication and group interaction which are of value in themselves and are known to be valued by employers outside higher education. It is desirable with small-group learning, as with any other flexible learning strategy, that it be introduced to students at an early stage in their degree programme. This will allow them the maximum scope to cultivate the skills which it fosters and help to allay anxieties which they may feel if they are subjected to abrupt alterations in their learning experience.

Projects and presentations

Two additional forms of flexible learning initiative which are associated with small-group learning are student presentations and *joint* project work. Student presentations can be of a relatively informal nature (as a follow-up to a small-group session for example) or they can be included in a module's assessment package and might involve the presentation of materials. If this latter option is pursued students can compile course folders consisting of each other's work, which can be an effective means of promoting a sense of group identity. Similarly, joint project work can provide the opportunity for students to pursue subjects in more detail and encourage independence, initiative and skills in cooperation, delegation, time-management and formative self-evaluation.

Debate and performance

One of the flexible learning strategies which has been found to be most efficacious in terms of facilitating productive seminar discussion within a large group (in excess of 20 students) is the organization of debating teams. This can take a variety of forms but has, in our experience, proven to be most effective when a group is divided into two teams expected to present antithetical cases. Each team is permitted approximately half of a meeting to construct their case, and the debate is chaired by a nominated 'neutral' student who will conclude the session with a summation. Along with the debate, performance of selected passages of poetry, prose and drama can be a means of diversifying the seminar format, one which increases participation and can provide a useful starting-point for discussion of texts and student preconceptions.

Flexible lectures

It should not be imagined that these flexible learning strategies are necessarily exclusive of traditional teaching practices such as the lecture. Lectures can still be an invaluable mechanism for the delivery of that subject information which is not often recognized as a vital component in an English degree. There is, however, no reason why a lecture cannot include a space for more interactive means of assimilating this information and thus off-set that deterioration across time of student concentration which research has shown to typify even the most 'lively' of lecturer performances. Lectures could, for example, include brief presentations/performances by students and a period of small-group work in which to apply new knowledge to specific texts and questions.

Implementing flexible approaches

In the course of implementing any of the flexible learning initiatives which I have sketched above we have found it useful to adopt the following four-step procedure: planning; briefing; resourcing; and assessment. The surest way of failing to establish a successful project is to indulge in spontaneous and *ad hoc* meddling. The first essential step in this process must involve careful forward planning which, in accordance with the machine-age folk adage that warns 'if it ain't broke, don't fix it', has to begin with an honest appraisal of current courses and teaching practice to determine which areas would actually benefit from modification. Once these decisions have been taken it is important, as mentioned earlier, that students are fully briefed about changes and are reminded of the mutual responsibilities of lecturers and learners in the consensual activity of flexible learning.

When it comes to the stage at which a project has to be resourced, lecturers invariably come face-to-face with the depressing logistics of learning in the 90s. However, while many flexible learning projects involve an initial outlay in terms of money and time, they can provide long-term advantages in relation to savings in staff time and improvements to the student learning experience. Resourcing should involve both the provision of the requisite new materials, which can be planned on an inter-departmental basis and involve student participation (worksheets, open-access files containing subject-specific information and guides to effective small-group and project work) and the utilization of currently available technological resources such as computer databases and audio-visual libraries. In the context of a transition to student-centred learning systems, one goal of a department's space strategy ought to be the maintenance or provision of an area on site within which small-group and project work can take place. The lay-out of teaching spaces may also require reorganization. There is no paradigm for the arrangement of a classroom, but it is certain that the traditional design (whereby the lecturer stands facing seated students) accentuates the 'them' and 'us' division and acts as a physical disincentive against the type of discussion *within* a group which flexible learning seeks to encourage.

Lecturers risk establishing a pedagogical inconsistency if flexibility is applied unilaterally to the delivery of courses and not considered in relation to their assessment. *'Flexible assessment'* can take a variety of forms: formal and informal, formative and summative, self-, peer- and lecturer-assessment. There is no reason to assume that student self-assessment, one of its most contentious forms, is an 'all-or-nothing' affair – it need not be part of the formal assessment process (although there are good reasons why it should be) to be of value in the task of teaching students how to recognize their weaknesses and develop their strengths. One relatively straightforward means of achieving this is the introduction of a form, to be submitted with all written work, in which students are invited to assess themselves in particular categories ('style', 'structure', 'focus', 'use of secondary materials', etc.) and to make general comments by way of conclusion. Lecturers can then enter their own assessment and comments alongside that of the student. As part of the process of the assessment, flexible learning projects themselves, particularly when they have been pilot schemes, require a thorough review. This can range from an informal consideration of the overall quality of written work and seminar discussion and a weekly diary recording the successes and failures of particular initiatives, to meetings with colleagues to discuss specific projects and the distribution of questionnaires for the student evaluation of courses on which flexible learning methods have been introduced.

Wider application across higher education

By the same token that, as was suggested at the outset, 'flexible learning' is more than simply a voguish rhetoric, it is also very far from being a panacea for the array of difficulties confronting English departments in the 90s. On its own, flexible learning cannot provide a satisfactory solution to or substitute for the problem of an inadequately funded university system. Therefore if we develop new procedures for 'student-centred learning' in the humanities they must be accompanied by a set of realistic expectations and achievable goals. Flexible learning may not have all the answers, but it can encourage us to ask important questions, not least about the experience of students in our departments. To ask such questions is not to call implicitly for a dramatic overhaul of current teaching methods, nor to call for the abandonment by lecturers of their role as providers of knowledge. Rather, it is to continue the process of constructing an educational environment which maximizes the degree of authentic participation by students in their own education, allowing them to fulfil their individual potentials and hopefully to enjoy themselves. A colleague within my department annually concludes the inaugural first year lecture with this salutary warning about education from Doris Lessing (Lessing, 1962, p. vii):

Ideally, what should be said to every child, repeatedly, throughout his or her school life is something like this:

'You are in the process of being indoctrinated. We have not yet evolved a system of education that is not a system of indoctrination. We are sorry, but that is the best that we can do.... Those of you who are more robust and individual than others will be encouraged to leave and find ways of educating yourself – educating your own judgement...'.

At its best flexible learning can offer lecturers in English more than just a means of struggling with deteriorating conditions and depleted resources. It can be a means of ensuring that our students are thoroughly 'indoctrinated' with the skills of independent critical intelligence. There is no reason why such a process of indoctrination should not occur in a range of disciplines across higher education.

References

Berryman, J (1972) 'Dream Song No. 14', *Selected Poems*, London: Faber and Faber.
Lessing, D (1962) *The Golden Notebook*, Harmondsworth: Penguin.

Part Three: The Student View of Flexible Learning

Chapter Fourteen

Student Opinion of Flexible Teaching and Learning in Higher Education

Richard Clark

Introduction: Investigating attitudes to innovatory teaching

Few higher education institutions appear to have developed open and formal arrangements for student-oriented discussion of teacher innovation. The common forum for discussion of teaching is usually the course or departmental staff-student liaison committees which are driven by quality audit and assessment procedures. They have for the most part encompassed a duality of purpose, providing feedback within a staff assessment environment and thus separating staff from students, rather than promoting partnership. Such consultative committees and student feedback questionnaires are inherently reactive, allowing students to complain but discouraging praise and innovation. The student community suffers, of course, from its powerlessness and transitory status. Even the most democratically governed committees can effectively stifle student discussion and there is practically no effective forum for student consultation in the process of course development. Faculty committees ratify or at best modify course proposals with student comment deferred to as an afterthought. The long time-lag between innovation and practice means that students rarely see the application of their input. There are few opportunities for the student community to actually engage in discussion on a partnership basis with their tutors.

It was with considerable trepidation therefore that in response to the Flexible Learning Initiative at Loughborough University, a survey of student opinion of projects from a number of academic departments was undertaken. This survey sought to encourage both praise and criticism and to assess the prospects for further development.

The aim of this study was to explore student opinion of teacher innovation in the following areas:

- satisfaction with flexible as compared with traditionally structured learning;
- factors making the development of flexible teaching less attractive to students and staff;
- the nature of special preparation and provision which might be needed in order to make the transition from conventional to flexible more fluid.

Methodology

This study was based upon structured interviews with the participants in the Flexible Learning Initiative projects involving the following departments: geography, English and drama, education, maths sciences, design and technology, and the Engineering Design Institute. To carry out this research, the university appointed an independent researcher with a background in student union representation. This move was taken to add credibility to the student interview process.

The project tutors were of course self-selected through their involvement in the pilot projects. In addition to providing background information on their projects the tutors were also pivotal in establishing links between the students and the researcher, helping in many instances to set up the student interviews, freeing room space and/or teaching time to allow the interviews to take place. Tutors invited cooperation from their project groups, and so the study was based on an opportunity sample of those expressing a willingness to participate.

The students interviewed came from the diverse range of courses and therefore do not form a consistent sample regarding year or stage of study. They came from undergraduate and postgraduate groups, on and off site, full and part course units. Similarly no attempt was made to construct a representative sample based upon age, sex or backgrounds of the students.

Student interview groups were organized within each department and limited in size to a maximum of six students representing a sample of between 10 and 20 per cent of the total. Although the students were told of the purpose of the interview and were invited to reflect upon their experiences, they were not required or given any chance to prepare for the interview itself. They were assured of confidentiality from the outset: although their cooperation was encouraged and invited, and therefore known by their tutor, their names were commonly not disclosed to the researcher. At no stage in the report process were individual comments attributed to names.

The first five minutes of the interview were occupied with the students completing a simple tick-box questionnaire exploring their experiences of diverse teaching techniques. This then formed the basis for the wider-ranging group discussion to follow. Interview time was set at half an hour. The interview discussions were recorded by hand during the interview with comments noted in full and written up within four hours of the interview.

We should finally consider the wider status of these student opinions.

Should they be seen as individual comments, or are they representative of a wider community? While some of the students clearly attempted to speak on behalf of their absent colleagues, their comments on the whole must be taken as personal, drawing wider assumptions carefully. It is also important to recognize that many of the students' opinions were formulated as a group, having been encouraged to reflect on each other's responses during the course of what, in effect, became an open discussion chaired by the researcher.

Broadly speaking the six groups interviewed had experienced two different aspects of flexible learning, namely self-guided study material, and group work. The results will be presented accordingly.

Ownership and empowerment through self-guided study

Students from the following departments were taught through self-guided study units for various course elements: education, maths sciences, design and technology, and the Engineering Design Institute.

Students gave a number of reasons for their liking of self-guided study. By far the most common, raised by every group involved in this way of working, was expressed as follows:

It's good in the way that its up to you. There aren't any deadlines and you work to your own pace.

This was explained as a release in pressure that students felt from their more traditional studies, a pressure arising from an emphasis upon assessment: 'Its not pass or fail, there's no pressure'. Students clearly felt that the ability to work *when and where* they wanted was a clear improvement on their wider study experiences.

This notion of self-motivation was strongly connected in their responses with that of self-determination of priorities. Of equal importance was the chance to apply personal learner objectives to their work habits: 'You can work to your own level'.

Obviously this ties in with the release of pressure to achieve beyond the minimal levels of competence set by (external) course requirements, and a student's personal level of subject competence. However, the students were also applying a commitment to each subject based on personal preference and/or priority. The 'own level' therefore applies to both the students' self-assessed level of subject confidence and to their level of priority.

If you want to look in deeper you can or you can skip it. Its important to be able to judge your own input on individual modules, to chose what's the most relevant to you.

This need to be in charge of their studies endorses the notions of student empowerment as discussed by several project tutors, encouraging the students to seize the materials and take ownership.

The actual provision of the materials was praised for facilitating successful learning. Welcoming the inbuilt flexibility that characterized the self-guided study materials, allowing the students to gauge their starting level based upon their previous experience, they felt that this was '...more realistic'. Such comments again indicate a watering down of the pressure of a more conventional 'all in' mass delivery, acknowledging the student diversity now characterizing higher education.

For one student the materials from the engineering design project provided a far more substantial opportunity to learn successfully than the offer of empowerment and responsibility. This student felt completely confident in his ability to recall the material and topics covered in the study guide as it would appear that the visual presentation and sequencing of the information closely matched his preferred way of taking pictorial/structured notes.

Perhaps the most easily overlooked advantage of developing innovative teaching within a more traditional teaching/learning environment is stated in the comment of one first year student who felt that the self guided approach, '... made a nice change'. The flexible learning projects were thus clearly placed within a wider context of conventional teaching delivery.

In a later section of the interviews, the students were asked to identify their preferences as learners. The most common response was a mixture of both conventional and innovative teaching techniques. The remainder of the students were equally divided between those students siding more strongly with either self-guided study or conventional delivery of lecture/tutorial.

The skills benefits of self-guided study

All of the student groups interviewed were able to articulate the main benefit of self guided work as being the chance to develop the skills of self motivation, discipline and time management:

You learn self-reliance, its all down to you
or,
You need to be able to sort yourself out.

One group of postgraduate students felt more confident in this area than the other groups, suggesting that post-experience students are more likely to have developed work/learner discipline. They also expressed a concern for undergraduates for whom it was felt that self-guided study would be a 'challenge'. Mature undergraduates also expressed concern for their colleagues from more traditional entry routes.

The demands of self-responsibility and time management were seen as having a beneficial influence on students' wider studies and study patterns. For many this was their first experience of such wide-ranging responsibility and empowerment, being more familiar with the demands of more conventional teaching. Arising from the general ability to manage their time, the students abstracted the ability to target and gauge their individual priorities. This was seen as having an important bearing on the 'own level, own pace' benefit of self-guided study as well as attaining a wider significance in the assessment of long-term targets and achievements. Of course, the process of establishing priorities means that some tutors will find themselves in the position of having their modules or pieces of work de-prioritized, as we shall see later.

The students were also able to identify specific study skills, perhaps of a more conventional nature. Those involved in the maths module welcomed the opportunity to develop 'book skills' through the combined use of closely structured study guides and textbook. This was welcomed as a change to their usual pattern of learning which was dependent upon tutorial- and lecture-based dissemination of information. This learner objective had been built into the development of the project and it is therefore additionally helpful to know that such objectives can be achieved and will be warmly acknowledged.

The advantages of group work

Students from the English and geography departments participated in group work rather than traditional seminars under tutor guidance.

By far the most beneficial aspect of group work, as strongly emphasized by both group work projects, was the area of skill development or the acquisition of specifically 'non-academic skills'. While this was partly seen as a satisfying educational end in itself, some students expanded these benefits to the wider context of future participation in the job market. This issue of 'employability' was most strongly emphasized by final-year geography students who were pressingly aware of the need to prove themselves at interviews. The relevance of group skills to external, non-academic, working practices was also strongly emphasized by design and technology students, for whom this was of high personal importance, although they were not directly involved in group work through the flexible learning initiatives.

Specific group-work skills identified by the students emphasized delegation and self analysis, asking such questions as: 'What approach would best work for our strengths?' Both project groups had warmly embraced the opportunity to target individual strengths and weaknesses and to arrange workloads accordingly, and both groups felt that they had used this skill stratification to achieve the optimum output. However, it was also seen as important that they avoid inter-group isolation of tasks and individuals. The student groups developed an awareness of the need to vary activities between small sub-groups and individuals within the wider group environment.

Delegation and the devolvement of responsibility encouraged students to embrace this responsibility and work to specific group deadlines:

I tend to leave everything to the last minute but you can't do this here, so it pushed me along and,

It was more difficult working in a group but the pressure was a lot better than drifting.

These students acknowledged and welcomed their responsibility to others, recognizing this as a successful and pleasing motivator, encouraging them to complete their work.

Another skill identified was that of giving and receiving feedback. Although it was commonly felt that this was a difficult skill to acquire and maintain under stressful conditions, the students felt encouraged by their, mostly negative, experiences:

I wasn't sure if I was ever going to speak to my friends again ... but these were the most lucid arguments we'd ever had.

The students' experience of internal group dynamics played an important part in eliciting praise for this way of working. The group environment was described as being 'safe' and 'supportive', allowing and encouraging individuals and groups to face new challenges and attain new skills and subject understanding. Support reduced the pressure on individuals, permitting them to attempt rather than retreat from challenging demands. The conclusion of such a response was that group work was ultimately praised for creating the potential for greater reward and overall attainment, particularly with regard to final assessment outcomes.

The disadvantages of group work

While both pilot project groups welcomed the potential skills benefit arising from their participation in group activity, they felt dramatically unprepared for the task at hand. Of primary importance to both groups were the difficulty of inter-group communication and the process of sharing and accepting responsibility.

An important element of this was trust – 'How do I know that the others will do the work?' Exploring this issue more fully, the students discussed a fear of compromising their own skills and targeted level of output. This worry was most strongly expressed by two mature students from separate projects who were anxious about 'carrying along' their younger colleagues: 'Mature students have more motivation'.

This fear of compromise was of course closely related to final assessment – 'What will it do to my marks?' – and was felt to be of particular concern in the subjective, opinion-oriented work of the English department:

We are individually encouraged to develop our own opinions, but group work encourages compromise and fence-sitting.

In all areas the students felt that significant prior experience of group work would help to relieve some of the tensions regarding assessment and the competition/compromise dilemma. Students involved in innovative group work called for a fully integrated group and individual learning environment right from the first year of undergraduate study. They were unanimous in stressing that if faced with similar demands for which they felt unprepared in the future, they would reject them in favour of competently handled lectures and tutorials: 'Give us back our lectures!'

An important though clearly separate skills shortage was perceived to exist among their tutors, namely the process of building student groups and the orchestration of group activity. Concern was expressed over the casual formation of 'accidental' groupings left over from previous group exercises. It was clearly felt that each group should be 'built' according to the individual exercise at hand and the particular strengths and weaknesses of the individual students. 'Accidental' groupings were seen as being 'stifling' and 'inappropriate'.

Many students expressed a fear that if a group 'went wrong' their marks would be severely damaged. While stressing the general potential for raising their marks, they were all too aware of the equal potential for disaster. The need for tutors to be able to assess and monitor group performance at an intermediate stage or stages and successfully intervene if and when appropriate, was seen as being vital to student confidence. Tutors should also be able to change groups around from task to task to reduce compartmentalization of weaknesses and tensions.

To spoonfeed or...?

Malcolm Cornwall (1988) writes of a series of hypothetical barriers to the introduction of flexible approaches to teaching and learning in a traditional institution of higher education based upon his own experiences. Two of these perceptions can be linked:

Most students prefer to be taught
and,
Students are not capable of working independently.

Put into contemporary language, these combine to present one of the principal prejudices against developing flexibility, that 'students just aren't what they used to be'. It is a common feeling in higher education today that students lack motivation and discipline, desiring only to be spoonfed. Such sentiments are also echoed by clearly well-intentioned staff, with several of the project tutors couching their opinions in terms of the educational integrity of promoting self-responsibility amongst learners.

This study has revealed several new angles on this belief. First, it is clear that all of the student groups interviewed identified and welcomed the potential for self-improvement arising from the new emphasis upon student autonomy. Second, it is also true that few of the students actually confessed to having the necessary skills. Even those students who were enthusiastic about the materials and had felt comfortably in control of their work, could not confidently acknowledge their ability to manage their own time and exercise self-discipline. Identifying the *need* for personal motivation, one postgraduate student asked, 'But isn't that something you're meant to grow into?'

Conversely the minority of students who did feel prepared and motivated, all post-experience and mostly postgraduate, would have preferred an alternative, more conventional method of delivery. This same group suggested that this method of learning may be more appropriate to undergraduate, 'traditional' students.

In conclusion there would appear to be a danger in drawing too simplistic a dividing line between traditional undergraduates and post-experience under- and post-graduates. However, we *can* draw some significant conclusions concerning the influences affecting the successful implementation of autonomous learning. In discussing their experience of teaching innovation, the students highlighted several key demotivators which restricted their successful development of autonomy, and it is these we shall discuss next.

Learner confidence

The most commonly experienced demotivator for all the groups interviewed was in the area of learner confidence. This can be most clearly expressed in the oft-repeated phrase, 'How do you know whether you're learning the right thing?'

This emphasis upon establishing and learning the 'right thing' was found at all levels, from first-year undergraduate to post-experience postgraduates, and in all courses from maths to English. These latter students found themselves looking for an authority figure in the form of a tutor to, '... put the discussion back on the right tracks'.

Even in the subjective study of literature it would appear that students still need the reassurance of the 'right' answer. Such a crisis of confidence was discussed on a variety of levels. From a different perspective, students involved with the study guides wanted to be led through more than one textbook to provide comparative views. One student was dissatisfied with solely preparing his own notes directly from a textbook and study guides, missing the handouts and other tutor inputs from lectures and tutorials. This wasn't as simple a matter as desiring to be spoonfed, for he went on to say:

I don't like making my own notes. You only get one set from the study guides and I prefer two sets to help me revise.

While having an obvious impact upon resources, this call for multiple referencing more closely mirrors, perhaps, the endless learner pursuit of the right answer rather than any inherent learner laziness. Even the most enthusiastic students on self-guided courses never felt truly satisfied, as shown in the testimony of a student from the famed McMaster Medical School in Canada (Ferrier *et al.*, 1988):

... with all the long hours and seclusion I still don't feel that I've accomplished anything near the learning I should have done so far.

Perhaps all too often tutors overlook the pressure to succeed arising out of an assessment-led culture. Similarly, tutors may also forget the 'novice-initiate' status of the student, possibly facing up to their learning for the first time. Do we need to switch from assessment-led training to learning-led education?

The students seemed to feel that this issue of learner confidence was best resolved, or at least that their concerns were best minimized, when their lack of confidence was addressed through periodical assessment and feedback. Without intermediate feedback one student described attaining an 'artificial sense of success and achievement' once the self-guided study material had been completed. This was echoed by several different students, expressing some degree of confusion over what they had actually done and achieved. It is important to not only assess the attainment of subject understanding but to validate the students' adopted strategy of work. Has the offer of autonomy paid off? Have the students successfully guided their own learning and assumed proper responsibility? How can a students' learning *process* be authenticated?

Interim assessment is seen as one important motivating factor, giving the 'leave everything to the last minute' brigade some intermediate focus points for their output. Feedback arising from assessment also gave the students reassurance, providing them with the confidence to proceed from one stage to the next. In a similar vein, several students praised the provision of interim tutorial sessions, providing them with 'live' validation of their individual work as well as opportunities to secure help should they need it. Overall, the self-guided course with the most structured contact time, utilizing lecture test and tutorial, was the combination most warmly welcomed by its students.

The issue of learner confidence also arose when discussing the benefits of 'own level, own pace'. Students felt unsure as to whether the inherent flexibility built into the study guides to cater for diverse previous experience would allow them to miss out important information. Conversely, would it be too easy for them to skip through, thus again inducing a superficial sense of success? Where it was clear that no right or wrong answer was available the students were thrown into some confusion over how easy it might be to cheat: 'Can we cheat by just ticking everything?'

The assessment/learner confidence conundrum was expressed in its most extreme form when students were asked about the pros and cons of the wider development of flexible approaches. The students clearly felt worried that an increased emphasis upon self-study, with the accompanying perception of an increased distance from a tutor, presented the danger of,

people getting behind without anyone knowing about their progress.

Similarly they express the fear that '... a lot of people will drop out'.

These remarks predominantly came from a group on a short-term, self-guided package with no interim assessment, who were preoccupied with this issue. The same group offered the opinion that,

no contact may mean no motivation to sort out your problems.

The role of tutor as motivator in the development of student autonomy is therefore an important one.

Related to this wider development of self-guided work were the concerns of a first-year group that if increased numbers of students from across the university were studying away from their departments, there would be problems with the overcrowding of halls of residence. If students are asked to work at home the traditional use of study rooms within halls becomes deeply problematized. Would this provide a suitable working environment? These students honestly outlined a plethora of distractions arising from an overpopulated hall during the day time, ranging from the noise of others to the ease of avoiding work – 'I think I'd rather play badminton'. The community living environment in this instance threatens individual study and limits access to quiet areas and times.

Student confidence also surfaced with the rather unexpected announcement made by one student that she did not feel confident in the self-guided material because she could not,

... mess about with them. I do all my work on the PC. But I couldn't even photocopy this and make mistakes and rearrange things.

The actual ownership of the materials and the perceived inability to personalize the document thus limited her confidence, effectively alienating her from the project. Inflexibility of this sort is thus another perceived demotivator, threatening already fragile learner confidence.

Other demotivators

Pivotal to the issue of student acceptance of teaching innovation was the issue of their wider current experience of teaching and learning in higher education. Two students had prior experience of flexible approaches, one from the Open University and the other from sixth-form college, but for the majority this was a new experience, finding a learner-oriented approach original and, to a lesser extent, challenging. For some this challenge was a welcome one: 'It made me get on with it', for others, less welcome: 'I felt intimidated and threatened'.

One interview group had reacted negatively to their whole project and while this cannot be taken to be representative of that entire area of development, it does point towards one of Rogers' basic principles of learning (1975):

Learning which involves a change in self organisation – in the perception of oneself – is threatening and tends to be resisted.

In rejecting the self-study materials this group was perhaps the most articulate in exploring their own weaknesses as learners, somewhat despairingly announcing their reliance on pressure and 'leaving everything to the last minute'. These students listed a series of challenges that, for whatever reason, they felt unable to accommodate, including unfamiliarity with assessment criteria, uncertainty of purpose and complete disregard of the tutor's perceived, and much hoped for, student empowerment.

As mentioned earlier, the impact of change itself cannot be underestimated. While the new approaches constituted a 'nice' change they were also seen in a wider focus as being 'too demanding'. It is often assumed that, like swimming, independence and discipline are learnt by being plunged into the water and offered a little guidance. However, the testimony of the students has confirmed that their fear and distrust of the 'plunge' will limit their cooperation with tutor-led innovations in teaching. If students are unsure about the motives for change, as well as the new ground rules for innovative teaching and learning, they will dig their heels in and resist change with frustration and obstinacy, perhaps suspecting the tutor's ulterior motives. Another of Rogers' prerequisites for learning summates this dilemma:

Those learnings which are threatening to the self are more easily perceived and assimilated when external threats are at a minimum (ibid., p.151).

Such threats can, as has been shown here, include the challenging of one's perceptions and expectations of higher education. This perhaps led to the post-experience students requesting conventional deliveries, such as lectures and tutorials. These students were also reacting to a need for change:

We direct our lives at work, we want something rather different from our education.

Another demotivator is the occasional lack of the learner confidence which can be gained from assessment and feedback. While the students were dismissive of informal assessment, they were generally in favour of small-scale periodic diagnostic assessment, affirming both subject attainment and work strategy, discussing this in terms of confidence to proceed. Learner confidence needs to be inspired by more than a chatty prose style or visual design.

Assessment was also seen as part of a partnership between staff and students. Put bluntly, it shows that the students aren't the only ones doing the work. For one student operating without intermediate opportunities for feedback, 'The time commitment alone warranted some form of feedback'.

Another group put this more firmly, having reacted against their tutor's initiatives. These students felt that they were being asked to do all the work and had not acknowledged the process of empowerment, initiated by the innovative change. The inherent danger in promoting flexible approaches as a chance to free-up contact teaching time is that the students will perceive this as a denigration of their educational experience, and revolt rather than cooperate.

Student priorities

In the dawning age of flexibility we need to acknowledge that having been offered the freedom to choose, students will want to exercise this right. This will involve saying no as well as yes. If we are to cater for individual prior experience and personal priorities we must accept that students will apply these to their studies and are indeed already doing so, in spite of the system rather than because of it. The student interviewees stressed several influences upon their personal priorities. Perhaps the most significant of these was an assessment of demand, asking two simple questions: 'What work does this involve?' and 'How does this relate to my other studies?'

"Demand' covers module weighting as well as intermediate assessment methodologies and other rewards. Differing methods of assessment from module to module mean that students are continually encountering assessment periods throughout their term of study, as opposed to the traditional end-of-term/end-of-year model of assessment. In this respect, tutors can not afford to view their module in isolation from the other demands being placed on each student. In a busy schedule, longer-term reward clearly attains high individual priority. In this context students were equally clear in their rejection of informal assessment, inevitably relegating its importance as a time-wasting exercise. Although assessment and feedback were identified as essential to the development of learner confidence, an emphasis upon assessment results in value judgements being made and priorities affirmed.

Weighting and reward seemed to drive the students more than personal interest, although perhaps now that they were studying on a module, their interest in the subject may have been assumed and not raised in discussion. While workload plays a role in the development of personal priorities, students, in expressing choice, will also develop a prioritized strategy based upon their own learner objectives and interests. Several of the pilot projects were dismissed as being 'uninteresting' or as having less relevance to their individual need, referring more to course content rather than the actual delivery of material.

Drawing conclusions

Learners and learner skills

Perhaps it would be useful to now place some of the student comment in a wider context, reflecting upon how these comments affect the wider implementation of teacher innovation within a traditional institution of higher education.

The most significant contributing factor to the 'give us back our lecture!' lobby was the perceived skills shortage experienced by students when faced with the new challenges presented by teacher innovation. While this was particularly true of the group work projects, it was also echoed by those dissatisfied with the self-guided study materials. Cornwall (1988, p. 246) puts this as follows:

Too often it seems, students and their teachers are plunged into new ways of teaching and learning on the assumption that they can pick up the new skills needed.

The group-work students felt unprepared to communicate and to negotiate delegation of responsibility successfully while the self-guided study groups particularly lacked the ability to motivate and manage their own time. The groups asked to make presentations were equally concerned that, '... students just do not know how to present information'. At no time had they been trained in the required skills and could only point to their various tutors as role models, a situation which was not seen as being particularly satisfactory.

Perhaps the most important lesson to be learnt here is that the rigours of developing innovative teaching place parallel demands upon those responsible for the learning. With innovative teaching comes innovative learning. Unfortunately, while we may pilot our teaching – either materials or method – it is perhaps impossible with current restraints to pilot learning, as bound as it is with the wider context of a student's entire programme of study.

It is common in higher education today to find programmes pushing the gradual and exploratory development of staff skills across the institution. As teacher innovation spreads across the institution, staff skill shortages are gradually being addressed as they become apparent, a fledgling strategy, which is, however, considerably more advanced than that for the development of the student community. The problem of developing teacher innovation within a more traditional institution is that the projects are clearly fixed, from the student perspective, within a wider context of conventional teaching and learning. This conventional context is of paramount status due to its longevity and its commonality, and does not provide students with the necessary skills and breadth of experience to meet new teaching and learning requirements. When students reject such innovation it confirms tutors' worries that they can no longer encourage or force their students to plunge into flexible learning on the grounds that they will either sink or swim. We need to be more proactive in empowering our students and equipping them with the skills necessary to take full and confident responsibility for their learning.

Students were equally articulate in their call for specific, timetabled opportunities for skills development, or a move towards rationalizing skill-specific learner objectives. Quoting the example of final-year students with 12 modules, one group felt that it was no longer appropriate for tutors to give out lengthy, unannotated reading lists. When they had pushed for some change through their course representative they were told that lengthy reading lists would do them no harm and were specifically devised to encourage the acquisition of research and information-gathering skills.

The students wanted to reject such a random approach due to time constraints, preferring such skills to be targeted at a specific area of work: 'I just haven't got the time to go through this again and again'.

Thus we can see that students are calling for two main developments in the wider context of teacher innovation. First, they want their skills short-age to be acknowledged and appropriate strategies implemented to rectify this. Second, any such strategy should be coherent, stating specified learner objectives, rejecting the more random sink-or-swim model of conventional strategy. Each institution and each course tutor needs to ask themselves where they are in developing such programmes.

This study has thrown up the need for training in group work and presentation skills alongside the delivery of more traditional skills such as note-taking and information-gathering. However, each new teaching style adopted will require a different configuration of skills, covering both conventional and more innovative areas. Practical training in specific skills would considerably boost student confidence and thus, perhaps, an accep-tance of flexible approaches to teaching. Indeed:

Study skills provision is a key factor in helping less confident learners across the transition from conventional to flexible learning (Moss, 1991, p.37).

Adequate skills training would also add a much called for vocational element to their studies, an element which might also fall into the personal prioritization and motivation framework through the delivery of possible and identifiable rewards.

Core or periphery?

How far can these changes go? The students were very clear in their answer to this question. When asked whether or not these innovations suited them, they were again unanimous in stating that:

It depends upon the difficulty of the module. This wasn't the most difficult and therefore I found it easier to relate to self-guided study. It also wasn't the most important.

Other students discussed the issue of centrality particularly relating to confidence in teaching technique:

It is good to experiment but it depends upon the particular subject. If a major area of work, you want the confidence of an established method of delivery. We need to know that it works.

There are, it would seem, 'suitable' and 'unsuitable' modules and areas of work, a statement echoed by the project tutors themselves. The most signif-icant factor in suitability would appear to be the proximity to the core of the particular subject area. Apart from English, and to a lesser extent, geogra-phy, the projects studied here were largely developed in supporting, rather than core, areas.

The relative key to the overall development of innovative teaching would appear to be the importance or status of the chosen subject matter. The chosen subjects cover background theory, practice and principle, preparing students for the main areas of work. Perhaps these are low-risk strategies adopted at the outset to avoid catastrophe. This procedure can be seen to be repeating itself. Many of the new projects submitted to the Flexible Learning Initiative office cover similar supportive areas of work such as basic drawing skills or remedial mathematics. Could these be the subjects no one wants to teach, as suggested by one project tutor, as they lack the glamour of weightier subject areas?

The student interviews also point to a wider pressure limiting the scope of change, namely the pressure to succeed. Students have invested large amounts of money as well as opportunity in their courses, perhaps rightly focusing on ongoing reward and final degree classification. The message is clearly that it is valid to experiment but the students need to know that it works where and when it matters. This concern can of course be mirrored in the attitudes of the course tutors themselves. Teaching is a very personal skill and, for many, methods will have been built up over a period of years. In this respect, learner and tutor concerns and confidence in new methodologies are of equal importance.

The validity of student review

In many ways the very inadequacy of this survey is evidence enough of the need for a greater emphasis upon student review. Perhaps there is also enough evidence to suggest that a closer, developmental relationship be initiated between staff and students.

The students involved in this study were honest and thorough in their discussions, proving to be as equally perceptive of their own weaknesses as learners as they were in offering insight into the strengths and weaknesses of the pilot projects themselves.

Those who have been involved with student course and student union representation will be all too familiar with the lack of discussion of teaching delivery and strategies for learning, the very thing that most closely binds students and staff together.

Conclusion

This study has raised many issues and where possible has tried to keep the student view paramount. We have discussed motivating factors, learner confidence, the urgent need for student skills development and the possible role of the new teacher. There are many barriers to change within traditional institutions of higher education and the potential for progress is partially increased through the sincere willingness and openness with which the students shared their opinions and experiences.

Such a reactive study as this has validity, if only to highlight the lack of more proactive dialogue, an absence made more dramatic by the development of innovative teaching techniques. While there is a need for more comprehensive studies, it should not overshadow the real issue of proactive consultation and empowerment.

In their book, *How Students Learn*, Entwistle and Hounsell (1975) describe the factors contributing to the development of new courses:

- knowing what we want the students to learn;
- some understanding of the different ways in which learning takes place;
- which teaching methods make use of various types of learning.

Equipped with this understanding tutors should be able to devise courses to meet these objectives. However, to continue with such one-sided development would appear to court disaster. The students in this study have confirmed that they have much to offer this equation, particularly focusing upon their motivations, preferences and priorities.

While students may not necessarily desire change, preferring the ease and comfort of established techniques, they are able to identify problems with innovative approaches. Furthermore, they have the insight to suggest recommendations to help rectify these problems. Students have much to offer in the development of teaching and learning in higher education. They have considerably more to offer than grumbling condemnation. They can speak with wisdom and insight when given the space and reason to do so.

References

Cornwall, M (1988) 'Putting it into practice: Promoting independent learning in a traditional institution', in Boud, D (ed.) *Developing Student Autonomy in Learning* (2nd edn), London: Kogan Page.

Entwistle, N and Hounsell, D (1975) 'How students learn: Implications for teaching in higher education', in Entwistle, N and Hounsell, D (eds) *How Students Learn*, Lancaster: Institute for Research and Development in Post-compulsory Education.

Ferrier, B, Marrin, M and Seidman, J (1988) 'Student autonomy in learning medicine: Some participants' experience', in Boud, D (ed.) *Developing Student Autonomy in Learning* (2nd edn), London: Kogan Page.

Moss, D (1991) 'School pupils' reactions to flexible learning', *British Journal of Educational Technology*, 22, 3.

Rogers, C (1975) 'Freedom to learn', in Entwistle, N and Hounsell, D (eds) *How Students Learn*, Lancaster: Institute for Research and Development in Post-compulsory Education.

Index

Items should be returned on or before the last date shown below. Items not already requested by other borrowers may be renewed in person, in writing or by telephone. To renew, please quote the number on the barcode label. To renew online a PIN is required. This can be requested at your local library.
Renew online @ **www.dublincitypubliclibraries.ie**
Fines charged for overdue items will include postage incurred in recovery. Damage to or loss of items will be charged to the borrower.

Leabharlanna Poiblí Chathair Bhaile Átha Cliath
Dublin City Public Libraries

Dublin City
Baile Átha Cliath

Date Due	Date Due	Date Due

The Teaching and Learning in Higher Education Series
Series Editor: John Stephenson

ETTIE'S ROAD TO THE RISING

The Palmerstown Papers

by Patricia Fogarty

Ettie's Road to the Rising

ISBN 978-1-911180-23-4

lettertec

Printed in Ireland by Lettertec